CODE TO CURE

DIGITAL THERAPEUTICS AND THE FUTURE OF PHARMA

CODE TO CURE

DIGITAL THERAPEUTICS AND THE FUTURE OF PHARMA

Subba Rao Chaganti

™ **PharmaMed Press**

An imprint of BSP Books Pvt. Ltd.

4-4-309/316, Giriraj Lane,

Sultan Bazar, Hyderabad - 500 001,

Telangana, India.

Code to Cure: Digital Therapeutics and the Future of Pharma
by Subba Rao Chaganti

Published by

™ **PharmaMed Press**

An imprint of BSP Books Pvt. Ltd.
4-4-309/316, Giriraj Lane, Sultan Bazar,
Hyderabad - 500 001, Telangana, India.
Phone: 040-23445688
E-mail: info@pharmamedpress.net
www.bspbooks.net/www.pharmamedpress.net

ISBN: 978-93-47311-14-7 (Paperback)

Disclaimer

Acknowledgements

No book is truly the work of one person. Though these pages carry my name, they are the result of countless conversations, inspirations, and supports that I am deeply grateful for.

First, I want to thank the many colleagues, industry peers, and students who asked the questions that sparked this book. Their curiosity—How do digital therapeutics fit into pharma? How do we market medicine that is made of code?—drove me to research, reflect, and ultimately write. Without their probing, this work may never have been conceived.

I am indebted to the experts and pioneers in digital health and pharmaceutical marketing whose work I studied and whose case studies fill these chapters. Companies like Pear Therapeutics, Akili Interactive, Propeller Health, Omada Health, Kaia, and others did not just create products; they created a new way of thinking about what medicine can be. Their stories gave this book its shape and its substance.

To my publisher, PharmaMed Press, and particularly Anil Shah, Nikunjesh Shah, and Naresh Daver, I extend my gratitude for their unwavering belief in the need for specialized literature in pharmaceutical marketing. Their encouragement has always been more than professional—it has been personal.

I also owe a deep thanks to my former students and young brand managers across India, the U.S., and beyond. Their hunger to learn, their willingness to challenge assumptions, and their eagerness to adapt to a changing industry gave me hope that the future of the pharmaceutical industry is in good hands.

To my family, my greatest source of strength:

My wife, Mahalakshmi, whose support and patience through long hours of writing made this work possible.

My children and their spouses—Srinivasa Phanindra, Geetha, Lavanya, Satya Shankara Aditya, Sowmya, and Chaitanya—who remind me constantly that knowledge is best used when shared.

And my grandchildren—Aditi, Eesha, Surya, and Shriya—who inspire me to continue learning, teaching, and imagining a future where healthcare is more compassionate and human.

Finally, I acknowledge the patients—those who are already using digital therapeutics, and those who will in the years to come. Their experiences are the real heart of this book. They remind us that innovation in pharma and technology is not about markets or margins, but about people—their struggles, their resilience, and their hope.

To all who contributed directly or indirectly: thank you. This book is for you, and because of you.

Subba Rao Chaganti

Preface

One evening not long ago, I read about a child with ADHD who was prescribed something astonishing—not a pill, not a counseling session, but a video game. His parents were skeptical, but within weeks, they noticed a change: he could focus longer on tasks, his attention drifted less, and his confidence grew. That game, EndeavorRx®, had been cleared by the FDA as the world's first prescription digital therapeutic for ADHD.

For me, that story captured in miniature what this book is about. Medicine is no longer confined to capsules and injections. Increasingly, it is found in algorithms, gamified interfaces, and smartphone apps. Code, once just a tool to support healthcare, is becoming healthcare itself.

This shift is not just scientific. It is commercial, cultural, and deeply human. It changes how patients experience care, how physicians prescribe, how regulators approve, and how pharma companies position themselves in an increasingly digital ecosystem. For marketers, it redefines what it means to build trust, demonstrate value, and engage patients in a meaningful way.

This book, Code to Cure: Digital Therapeutics in Pharma Marketing, is my attempt to map that transformation. It blends research with real-world examples, case studies with strategic frameworks, and above all, stories that illustrate the profound ways digital therapeutics are reshaping medicine.

I have written it for brand managers, students, healthcare professionals, and anyone curious about the future of pharma. I hope that you will come away not only with a better understanding of digital therapeutics, but also with a vision of their potential: to make healthcare more continuous, more personalized, and more human.

Because if a child's therapy can come in the form of a video game, then perhaps the future of medicine is not just about new molecules. It is about new possibilities. And it is a future already unfolding.

Subba Rao Chaganti

Contents

Appendices

Chapter 1

Introduction to Digital Therapeutics

In 2017, a patient struggling with substance use disorder walked out of a clinic with a prescription that would have been unimaginable a decade earlier. It wasn't for methadone. It wasn't for an anti-craving pill. It was for an app.

The app, reSET®, guided the patient through cognitive behavioral therapy exercises, delivered reminders and reinforcement, and kept him engaged between appointments. Weeks later, he was still abstinent—something that traditional therapy alone often failed to achieve. For the first time, code had become cure.

That moment wasn't just a novelty. It was the birth of a new therapeutic category: digital therapeutics (DTx).

From Molecules to Code

For centuries, medicine has been defined by the physical. Pills, syringes, scalpels—objects we could hold, measure, dispense. Digital therapeutics upend that assumption. They are evidence-based software interventions designed to treat, manage, or prevent disease.

Like drugs, they undergo clinical trials. Like medical devices, they require regulatory approval. Like both, they can be prescribed and reimbursed. But unlike anything before them, their raw material is software—algorithms, modules, and interactive designs that reshape behavior and outcomes.

Examples already exist across a spectrum of conditions:

Somryst®, delivering digital CBT-I for insomnia, helps patients fall asleep faster and stay asleep longer.

EndeavorRx®, a prescription video game, improves attention in children with ADHD.

Omada Health, a program for diabetes prevention, reduces risk through coaching, feedback, and behavioral nudges.

Each is different in form, but they share a defining principle: clinical proof. They don't just inspire wellness—they deliver measurable outcomes.

The Evolution: From Tracking to Therapy

To understand digital therapeutics, it is helpful to examine their origins.

The first wave of digital health was about tracking. Pedometers counted steps. Calorie apps logged meals. Sleep monitors measured restlessness. They offered visibility, but not therapy.

The second wave was about guidance. Apps like MyFitnessPal and Headspace coached users toward healthier habits. They changed behavior, but without clinical rigor or regulatory oversight.

Digital therapeutics represent the third wave. They take those same digital tools and hold them to the same standards as medicine—randomized controlled trials, peer-reviewed studies, and regulatory scrutiny. Where Fitbit tracks and Headspace guides, reSET and Somryst treat.

Drawing the Line: Apps vs. Therapeutics

It's easy to confuse a wellness app with a digital therapeutic—they both live on your phone, both send reminders, and both encourage change. But the difference is as sharp as that between a self-help book and a prescription drug.

- Headspace calms millions with meditation, but it is not FDA-approved and cannot claim to treat anxiety.
- Somryst®, by contrast, is tested, regulated, and prescribed for insomnia.
- Fitbit gamifies activity, but no doctor prescribes it for obesity.
- reSET® has been proven in trials to improve abstinence rates in substance use disorder and gained FDA approval.

The difference comes down to three things: evidence, regulation, and reimbursement. Digital therapeutics prove themselves through trials, win approval from regulators, and gain legitimacy when insurers agree to pay for them. Wellness apps don't.

Why they Matter: Filling the Gaps in Healthcare

The question then becomes: why do we need digital therapeutics at all? Isn't medicine already advanced enough?

The answer lies in the cracks medicine has never been able to fill.

- Diabetes: Drugs lower glucose, but they don't change diet. Omada Health addresses the behavioral gap by coaching patients daily.
- Depression: Medication helps, but therapy access is scarce. Deprexis offers digital CBT modules, closing the access gap.
- Asthma and COPD: Inhalers work—if patients use them. Propeller Health tracks usage, provides reminders, and improves adherence.

These aren't small problems. They're the everyday failures that turn effective medicine into ineffective outcomes. Digital therapeutics don't replace drugs. They reinforce, extend, and complete them.

Closing Thought

When medicine is dispensed, it often stops at the pharmacy counter. Digital therapeutics pick up where prescription medicine ends—guiding patients through the complex realities of daily life. They don't exist to compete with pills, but to stand alongside them, filling in the blind spots where biology alone is not enough.

What began with a pedometer on a waistband and a meditation app on a phone has now become something larger: software that doesn't just track or guide, but treats.

As reSET showed in 2017, the most powerful prescription may not come in a bottle—but in a download.

1.1 What are Digital Therapeutics?

In 2017, a 28-year-old patient struggling with substance use disorder left his clinic with an unusual prescription. It wasn't for methadone or naltrexone. It wasn't even for a pill. Instead, it was for a mobile app. The patient downloaded reSET®, a program built on cognitive behavioral therapy modules, and began working through exercises each day. Within weeks, he reported fewer cravings and stronger adherence to his recovery plan.

For centuries, medicine has been defined by the physical—pills in blister packs, syringes in refrigerators, devices strapped to the body. Digital therapeutics (DTx) challenge that definition. They are software-based interventions that treat, manage, or prevent diseases with the same clinical rigor as drugs or devices.

The Core Idea

At their heart, digital therapeutics are evidence-based software programs. They're not health-tracking apps or step counters. They must demonstrate efficacy in clinical trials, often undergo regulatory review, and may be prescribed and reimbursed in the same manner as traditional therapies.

Think of them as the next therapeutic modality—joining drugs, biologics, and devices. But instead of chemistry or hardware, their raw material is code.

Examples in Action

- Insomnia (Somryst®)

  Cognitive Behavioral Therapy for Insomnia (CBT-I) is effective but hard to access. Somryst digitized CBT-I, delivering structured sleep therapy through an app. In clinical trials, patients fell asleep more quickly, stayed asleep longer, and maintained their improvements months later. What once required a specialist is now accessible on a smartphone.

- ADHD (EndeavorRx®)

  When Akili Interactive launched EndeavorRx, parents were astonished. The therapy resembled a video game—complete with bright visuals, obstacles, and challenges. But behind the gameplay were algorithms designed to target attention pathways in the brain. Following trials that demonstrated measurable improvements in focus, the FDA approved it as the first prescription video game for children with ADHD.

- Diabetes (Omada Health)

  Managing diabetes isn't just about glucose—it's about daily behaviors. Omada Health's digital therapeutic combines coaching, data tracking, and behavioral nudges to prevent and manage Type 2 diabetes. Studies have shown that participants reduced their weight, improved glycemic control, and lowered long-term healthcare costs.

Why they Matter?

Traditional drugs address the biochemical side of disease. Digital therapeutics address the behavioral, psychological, and access gaps that drugs alone cannot fix. They deliver therapy in the spaces where patients live their lives—in kitchens, bedrooms, offices, and commutes—rather than only in clinics.

The power of DTx is not that it replaces medicine. It's that they expand it. They make therapy continuous, personalized, and responsive in ways that pills never could.

Closing Thought

When a doctor prescribes software instead of a pill, it feels almost counterintuitive. However, that is precisely the point: digital therapeutics challenge our assumptions about what therapy entails. They ask us to accept that a well-designed algorithm, grounded in science and validated by evidence, can be just as therapeutic as a drug.

And if the patient who once relied on a prescription bottle now finds healing through a prescription download, it may be time to redefine what we mean by medicine.

1.2 The Evolution of Digital Health Solutions

In 2009, a Silicon Valley engineer strapped a pedometer to his waistband, not because his doctor told him to, but because he was curious. Every beep, every count of his steps, gave him a small surge of motivation. That curiosity soon gave rise to Fitbit, one of the first devices to make health data personal, portable, and engaging.

It was a small leap at the time—counting steps is hardly therapy—but it planted a seed. If measuring behavior could influence it, could software one day treat behavior-driven disease?

That question set digital health on an evolutionary path that would eventually lead to digital therapeutics.

From Tracking to Guiding

The first wave of digital health was about measurement. Step counters, calorie trackers, sleep monitors—they gave people visibility into habits they often ignored. But measurement alone rarely changed outcomes.

The second wave was about guidance. Apps like MyFitnessPal or Headspace didn't just measure—they coached, encouraged, and built habits. Yet, while they improved wellness, they didn't undergo the gauntlet of clinical trials or regulatory scrutiny. They were tools, not therapies.

The leap to digital therapeutics occurred when innovators asked: What if we apply the behavioral science behind these tools to the same standards as medicine?

The First Digital Prescriptions

That leap became real in 2017 with Pear Therapeutics 'reSET®, the first FDA-approved prescription digital therapeutic. Unlike a wellness app, it had randomized controlled trial data proving its efficacy in substance use disorder. It wasn't just guidance. It was therapy.

Germany accelerated this shift with its DiGA Fast-Track program, which allowed certain digital health apps to be prescribed and reimbursed. Solutions like HelloBetter (for depression and anxiety) and Kaia Health (for chronic pain) proved that digital health could move beyond lifestyle and into mainstream medicine.

Paving the Way: The Role of Consumer Tech

Ironically, it was consumer tech that made this leap possible. The smartphone ensured constant access. Wearables like the Apple Watch and Dexcom's continuous glucose monitors made real-time data collection seamless. Cloud computing enabled storage and analytics at scale.

Without these foundations, digital therapeutics would have remained theory. With them, they became practice.

The Lesson

The evolution of digital health is a story of progressive ambition:

- First, measure (pedometers, calorie counters).
- Then, motivate (wellness apps, guided meditation).
- Finally, medicate (digital therapeutics validated by trials and regulators).

Each step built trust. Each step pushed the boundary of what "health through technology" could mean.

Closing Thought

The pedometer didn't cure the disease. But it nudged millions to walk more. The wellness app didn't require FDA approval. But it made mindfulness mainstream. These early tools were not the destination, but the bridge.

They set the stage for a more radical idea—that software itself could be therapy. And in that sense, digital therapeutics are not a rupture with digital health. They are its inevitable next chapter.

1.3 Differentiating Digital Therapeutics from Digital Health and Wellness Apps

On the surface, a wellness app and a digital therapeutic can look strikingly similar. Both live on your phone. Both offer daily reminders, interactive modules, and even soothing visuals. But the difference between them is the difference between a cookbook and a prescription—one inspires healthier living, the other is designed to treat disease.

Headspace vs. Somryst

Take Headspace, one of the world's most popular meditation apps. Millions of users swear by its calming voices and guided sessions. Studies suggest it reduces stress and improves focus. However, Headspace is not regulated, not prescribed, and not reimbursed by insurance providers. It is a wellness tool, valuable but optional.

Now contrast that with Somryst, a prescription digital therapeutic for insomnia. Built on Cognitive Behavioral Therapy for Insomnia (CBT-I), it underwent randomized controlled trials, submitted clinical data to the FDA, and earned approval as a bona fide treatment. Physicians prescribe it. Insurers reimburse it. Patients don't just use it for "better sleep"—they use it to treat a clinical disorder.

This is the dividing line: apps promise; therapeutics prove.

Fitbit vs. reSET®

Consider Fitbit. It transformed how millions engage with fitness by counting steps, logging sleep, and gamifying activity. But no regulator oversees its claims. It's designed for motivation, not for managing chronic disease.

Now consider reSET®, the first FDA-approved digital therapeutic for substance use disorder. Its clinical trials showed significantly higher abstinence rates compared to standard care. Like a drug, it had to prove efficacy and safety before it reached patients. Unlike Fitbit, it is prescribed by physicians and often reimbursed by payers.

Both are digital, both are health-related—but one focuses on lifestyle, while the other is medicine.

The Three Distinctions

Digital therapeutics differ from digital health and wellness apps in three crucial ways:

1. Evidence: DTx must demonstrate clinical efficacy through rigorous studies. Wellness apps may cite user satisfaction, but not randomized trials.
2. Regulation: DTx undergoes approval by authorities like the FDA or EMA. Wellness apps launch directly in app stores.
3. Reimbursement: DTx can be prescribed and reimbursed like drugs. Wellness apps rely on consumers paying out of pocket.

Why the Difference Matters

The distinction is not academic—it determines trust. A physician may recommend a wellness app as a complement to care, but they prescribe a digital therapeutic as treatment. A payer may cover a DTx because it lowers hospitalizations or relapse rates. A regulator ensures that a product is safe and effective before it reaches patients.

Wellness apps can inspire. Digital therapeutics must deliver.

Closing Thought

It is tempting to blur the lines between digital health and digital therapeutics—after all, both leverage technology to improve well-being. But the difference lies in the stakes. If a wellness app fails, the user shrugs and deletes it. If a digital therapeutic fails, a patient suffers.

That's why one is marketed as a lifestyle and the other is regulated as a medicine. And it's why digital therapeutics represent not just a new category of apps, but a new category of therapy altogether.

1.4 The Rationale behind Digital Therapeutics: Addressing Unmet Needs in Healthcare

In 2015, a man in rural Montana was diagnosed with depression. His doctor prescribed medication but also recommended therapy. The problem? The nearest psychiatrist was a three-hour drive away, and the wait time for an appointment was four months. For him, therapy wasn't just expensive—it was inaccessible.

This story isn't unusual. Across chronic and mental health conditions, medicine often delivers the drug but fails to deliver the supporting care. That gap—between what medicine prescribes and what patients actually experience—is where digital therapeutics step in.

The Behavior Gap: Diabetes and Daily Choices

Take Type 2 diabetes. Physicians can prescribe metformin or insulin, but medication alone cannot undo years of dietary habits or sedentary lifestyles. The real challenge lies in the "last mile" of care—helping patients make healthier decisions each day.

This is what Omada Health recognized. Their digital therapeutic combines connected devices, coaching, and behavioral nudges. Patients receive real-time feedback on their food, activity, and glucose levels, along with a personalized plan that adapts as they progress. Clinical studies show it reduces the risk of progression to full-blown diabetes.

The unmet need wasn't a lack of drugs—it was a lack of behavioral reinforcement. Omada filled that gap.

The Access Gap: Depression and Geography

Mental health offers another example. Access to therapy is uneven at best and impossible at worst. In some regions, patients face months-long waits for therapists; in others, stigma prevents people from seeking help at all.

Deprexis, a digital therapeutic for depression used in Europe, bridges this gap. Delivered entirely online, it provides structured cognitive behavioral therapy modules. Patients log in when needed, regardless of their location or the availability of specialists. Trials show significant symptom reduction compared to control groups.

The unmet need wasn't a lack of treatments—it was a lack of reach. Deprexis solved for access.

The Adherence Gap: COPD and Asthma

Even when drugs are available, patients often don't take them as prescribed. For conditions like COPD or asthma, adherence to inhalers can be inconsistent, leading to flare-ups and hospitalizations.

Propeller Health addressed this problem with a simple yet powerful solution: a digital sensor that attaches to inhalers, tracking usage and linking it to environmental triggers. Patients get reminders, and doctors get adherence data. The result? Fewer hospital visits, better self-management, and measurable cost savings.

The unmet need wasn't a lack of drugs—it was a lack of adherence. Propeller closed that gap.

The Lesson

Digital therapeutics are not trying to replace medicine. They are trying to repair its blind spots.

- Where drugs can't fix behavior, DTx can.
- Where geography blocks access, DTx can.
- Where adherence falters, DTx can.

They target the invisible moments in a patient's life—the choices, lapses, and barriers that often decide whether treatment succeeds or fails.

Closing Thought

The rationale behind digital therapeutics is deceptively simple: healthcare is more than prescribing. It is about living with a condition, day in and day out. And in those daily moments, pills often fall short.

Digital therapeutics meet patients where they are—on their phones, in their homes, in their habits—and offer what medicine alone cannot: constant, personalized, behavioral reinforcement.

That is why they exist. And that is why, increasingly, they matter.

Chapter 2

The Role of Digital Therapeutics in Healthcare Management

On a cold Tuesday morning in Manchester, a man with Type 2 diabetes wakes up, checks his phone, and sees more than the weather forecast. His screen displays his predicted blood sugar curve for the day, offers a reminder to take his medication, and suggests a lighter breakfast option to help keep his glucose steady. By the time he leaves home, he has already received more real-time care than he would from a clinic visit.

This quiet transformation illustrates the role digital therapeutics (DTx) are beginning to play: not as replacements for doctors or drugs, but as continuous companions—managing, nudging, and guiding patients through the daily realities of living with disease.

Enhancing Patient Outcomes

Medicine has always been haunted by a simple truth: the best therapy fails if patients don't stick with it. Non-adherence—patients forgetting pills, skipping therapy, or abandoning lifestyle changes—costs billions every year and, more importantly, costs lives.

Digital therapeutics address this head-on. By embedding behavioral science into interactive design, they enhance adherence, maintain patient engagement, and reinforce therapy between appointments.

A patient with insomnia, for example, may abandon sleep hygiene advice after a week. But with Somryst®, they receive structured, evidence-based cognitive behavioral therapy on their phone, night after night. Clinical trials demonstrated not only short-term improvements in sleep but also sustained outcomes over several months. The lesson? DTx doesn't just deliver therapy—they make therapy stick.

Treating a Broad Spectrum of Conditions

One of the surprises of digital therapeutics has been their range. They're not confined to one disease category; they touch almost every domain where behavior matters.

- EndeavorRx®: the world's first prescription video game, designed to improve attention in children with ADHD. Children play, but the gameplay is the therapy.
- Deprexis: an online cognitive behavioral program for depression, used widely in Europe, expanding access where psychiatrists are scarce.
- Kaia Health: a digital therapeutic for chronic back pain, blending physical therapy, mindfulness, and education through an app—with trials showing comparable outcomes to in-person therapy.

The common thread isn't the disease. It's the role of behavior. Wherever patient behavior influences outcomes, digital therapeutics can play a role in intervention.

Integration with Traditional Therapies

The question often arises: are digital therapeutics meant to replace drugs and in-person therapy? The answer, more often than not, is no. They are meant to augment.

A patient with COPD may continue using an inhaler, but with Propeller Health's inhaler sensor, both they and their doctor can track adherence and environmental triggers. A patient on antidepressants might also use a digital therapeutic delivering daily cognitive exercises, reinforcing biochemical treatment with behavioral support.

This isn't an "either/or" world. It's a "both/and" world—where digital therapeutics expand the therapeutic toolkit, complementing traditional care with continuity and personalization.

Case Studies: Managing Chronic Disease

The impact of this integration is most evident in chronic disease management, where long-term success depends as much on daily behavior as on medication.

- **Omada Health:** Their diabetes prevention program combines coaching, connected devices, and behavioral nudges. Clinical studies have shown that it reduces weight, improves glycemic control, and delays disease progression.

- **Propeller Health:** By monitoring inhaler use and linking it to triggers, they've reduced hospital visits for asthma and COPD, while empowering patients with actionable insights.
- **Kaia Health:** Their back pain app has scaled globally, offering low-cost, accessible therapy backed by evidence—an option for patients who otherwise face long wait times or high costs for in-person care.

These examples reveal the pattern: digital therapeutics thrive not in acute care, but in the everyday trenches of chronic disease, where habits, lapses, and behaviors make or break outcomes.

Closing Thought

Hospitals and clinics are centers of excellence, but they are not where health happens. Health happens in kitchens, bedrooms, workplaces, and commutes—far from the doctor's office.

Digital therapeutics extend care into those spaces. They don't just treat conditions; they help patients live with them. They bridge the gap between prescriptions and practices, between clinical advice and daily adherence.

And in doing so, they shift healthcare management from being episodic and reactive to continuous and proactive.

That is their quiet revolution.

2.1 Enhancing Patient Outcomes Through Digital Therapeutics

In 2003, the World Health Organization published a startling statistic: in developed countries, only 50% of patients with chronic diseases adhered to their prescribed treatments. That single number explained why so many promising therapies failed in practice—because patients often did not take them as intended. The WHO called it "the world's other drug problem."

Two decades later, digital therapeutics are emerging as one of the most promising solutions to this age-old issue. Their promise is simple yet profound: if medicine is only as effective as the patient's ability to use it, then therapy must be integrated with the patient, not just at the pharmacy counter.

Making Therapy Stick: The Case of Insomnia

Insomnia isn't just about sleepless nights—it is about the toll those nights take on work, mood, and health. For years, doctors prescribed sleeping pills, which offered temporary relief but little long-term solution. Cognitive Behavioral Therapy for Insomnia (CBT-I) proved more effective, but therapists trained in CBT-I are rare.

Enter Somryst®, the first FDA-approved digital therapeutic for insomnia. Delivered via smartphone, it guides patients through structured CBT-I modules. Clinical trials showed that patients fell asleep faster, woke up less at night, and maintained improvements for months, even after they completed the program.

Here, digital therapeutics didn't just replicate therapy. They made it scalable, accessible, and sustainable—turning proven science into lasting outcomes.

Reinforcing Behavior: Diabetes and Daily Decisions

For patients with Type 2 diabetes, the challenge isn't knowing what to do—it's doing it every day. Diet, exercise, medication adherence, stress—all shape outcomes more than prescriptions alone.

Omada Health recognized this and developed a digital therapeutic that combines connected devices, coaching, and personalized nudges. Patients received real-time feedback on glucose levels, diet, and activity. In clinical studies, Omada participants lost weight, improved their glycemic control, and reduced their risk of developing type 2 diabetes.

The key wasn't new medicine—it was reinforcing behavior at scale.

Sustaining Recovery: Substance Use Disorder

Substance use disorder has one of the highest relapse rates in medicine. Traditional care often stops at detox and clinic visits, leaving patients vulnerable to cravings in the weeks and months that follow.

reSET®, developed by Pear Therapeutics, tackled this gap. By digitizing cognitive behavioral therapy, it kept patients engaged daily, offering structured exercises and real-time reinforcement. Clinical trials showed significantly higher abstinence rates compared to standard care alone.

For these patients, digital therapeutics extended recovery beyond the clinic—into the fragile everyday spaces where relapse often begins.

The Lesson

The real test of medicine isn't what happens in the clinic. It's what happens when the patient leaves.

- Somryst® proved therapy could persist night after night.
- Omada Health proved that coaching could guide everyday decisions.
- reSET® proved engagement could sustain recovery.

Each example highlights the same principle: digital therapeutics enhance outcomes not by replacing medicine, but by ensuring medicine is lived, practiced, and sustained in real life.

Closing Thought

The difference between "good science" and "good outcomes" has always been behavior. Digital therapeutics close that gap. They are the bridge between what doctors prescribe and what patients actually do—between medical possibility and patient reality.

And in that bridge lies their true power: the ability to transform treatment from something episodic into something enduring.

2.2 The Spectrum of Conditions Addressed by Digital Therapeutics

When people first hear about digital therapeutics, they often envision something narrow—perhaps a diabetes app or a sleep tracker with additional features. But the reality is far broader. What began as a niche experiment has spread across conditions as varied as ADHD, chronic pain, substance use disorder, and depression.

The common thread isn't the disease itself—it's behavior. Wherever patient behavior influences outcomes, digital therapeutics have found fertile ground.

Rewiring Attention: ADHD and EndeavorRx®

In 2020, parents of children with ADHD were handed an astonishing prescription: a video game. EndeavorRx, developed by Akili Interactive, looked playful—featuring spaceships, challenges, and points. But beneath the surface, its algorithms were designed to stimulate and retrain neural pathways associated with attention.

After clinical trials involving over 600 children, the FDA approved it as the first prescription video game. The lesson was startling: therapy could be engaging, enjoyable, and still clinically validated. In ADHD, where medication helps but doesn't always solve attention deficits, EndeavorRx® opened a new therapeutic frontier.

Managing Chronic Pain: Kaia Health

Back pain is the leading cause of disability worldwide. Traditional treatment—physical therapy—works, but access is limited and costly. Kaia Health digitized this approach, combining guided exercises, education, and mindfulness through an app.

In trials, Kaia's program proved as effective as in-person therapy. For patients, it meant therapy without waiting lists, travel, or high costs. For healthcare systems, it meant scalable treatment for millions. Here, digital therapeutics tackled not only pain but also the inequity of access.

Fighting Relapse: Substance Use Disorder and reSET®

Relapse is the shadow that haunts recovery from substance use disorder. Traditional care provides clinic-based therapy, but patients relapse in the spaces between visits.

reSET®, Pear Therapeutics' pioneering product, digitized cognitive behavioral therapy and made it available anytime, anywhere. Clinical studies showed improved abstinence rates and treatment retention. By filling the void between clinic and daily life, reSET® addressed the reality of relapse—the gap traditional medicine left unguarded.

Scaling Mental Health: Deprexis

Depression is among the most prevalent conditions worldwide, yet millions never access therapy due to cost, stigma, or geography. In Europe, Deprexis emerged as a digital therapeutic that delivers online CBT modules. Patients complete structured exercises at their own pace, guided by evidence-based frameworks.

Trials demonstrated significant symptom reduction. More importantly, it reached patients who would have never otherwise seen a therapist. In mental health, where unmet need dwarfs available supply, digital therapeutics created access at scale.

The Lesson

From ADHD to back pain, from depression to diabetes, digital therapeutics are proving versatile. Organ systems or drug categories don't confine them. Their unifying principle is simpler: disease is shaped by behavior, and behavior can be changed through targeted software interventions.

Where medicine meets behavior, digital therapeutics step in. And because nearly every chronic or mental health condition has a behavioral component, its spectrum is vast.

Closing Thought

We once thought of therapy as something delivered in pills or sessions. Today, it can be accessed through games, apps, wearables, or interactive modules—each of which is clinically validated and targets a different condition.

The diversity of digital therapeutics is not a sign of scatter. It is a sign of potential. They are not one solution for one problem, but a new modality for many.

And in that breadth lies their most powerful promise: to transform not just one corner of healthcare, but the very definition of therapy itself.

2.3 Integration with Traditional Therapies: Complementary and Alternative Use Cases

For most of medical history, treatments came in binaries: either you took a drug or you didn't; either you saw a therapist or you didn't. Digital therapeutics blur that line. They don't ask patients to choose between traditional medicine and software—they amplify one with the other.

The genius of digital therapeutics is not in replacing what already works, but in reinforcing it, extending it, and sometimes even rescuing it.

Asthma and COPD: The Propeller Model

A patient with asthma leaves the clinic with an inhaler, which, when used correctly, effectively controls symptoms. But "when used correctly" is the catch. Inhalers are often left unused or used improperly.

Propeller Health attaches a small digital sensor to inhalers that records every puff, tracks adherence, and even links usage to environmental triggers such as pollen or pollution. The data is shared with physicians, who can spot patterns, adjust treatment, and intervene before emergencies.

Here, the inhaler remains the therapy. The digital overlay makes it effective. Propeller didn't replace the drug—it made the drug work better.

Depression: Pills Plus Programs

For patients with depression, antidepressants can rebalance neurochemistry, but medication alone rarely addresses thought patterns that sustain the condition. That's why cognitive behavioral therapy (CBT) is often recommended alongside drugs. The problem? Limited access to therapists.

Digital therapeutics, such as Deprexis, fill this gap. A patient may continue medication, but the app provides structured CBT exercises daily. Together, the drug addresses the biology while the digital therapeutic addresses the behavior.

This "both/and" approach transforms outcomes. The pill stabilizes mood. The program strengthens coping. Integration, not substitution, drives results.

Chronic Pain: The Kaia Blend

Chronic back pain patients are often caught between opioids (with their risks) and physical therapy (with its access barriers). Kaia Health offers a third option: digital physical therapy through its app.

But here's the nuance: Kaia is not positioned as a standalone cure. Many patients still use pain medication, see physicians, or attend occasional in-person therapy. Kaia ensures continuity—daily reinforcement, structured exercises, and mindfulness practices that complement everything else.

The result? Fewer flare-ups, reduced opioid dependence, and better long-term management.

The Lesson

Digital therapeutics are amplifiers, not adversaries. They rarely replace drugs, devices, or in-person care. Instead, they make each more effective by addressing behavior, adherence, and continuity.

- Drugs work more effectively when patients take them as prescribed.
- Therapy is more effective when patients can access it daily.
- Devices work better when usage patterns are visible.

DTx weaves itself into the fabric of existing care, closing the gaps between prescriptions and outcomes.

Closing Thought

The history of medicine is replete with innovations that initially emerged as competitors but ultimately evolved into complements. Stethoscopes didn't replace doctors; they amplified their ability to diagnose. Digital therapeutics are following the same path.

They are not asking medicine to step aside. They are offering to walk alongside—making every pill, every inhaler, every appointment more powerful by filling in the spaces in between.

That is their quiet but transformative role: not to replace medicine, but to complete it.

2.4 Case Studies: Successful Implementation in Chronic Disease Management

Chronic diseases are the marathon of medicine. They don't flare in emergencies; they grind away in daily life—slowly, relentlessly, often invisibly. And it's here, in the trenches of everyday choices and behaviors, that digital therapeutics have proven their worth.

The best way to see their impact is through stories—real-world cases where software stepped into the patient's life and quietly rewrote the trajectory of disease.

Omada Health: Preventing Diabetes One Decision at a Time

A 42-year-old woman in Texas with prediabetes knew her risk of developing Type 2 diabetes was high. Her doctor urged her to lose weight and exercise, but advice alone rarely translates into action.

Omada Health offered something different: a digital therapeutic combining connected scales, activity tracking, and real-time coaching. Every week, she uploaded her progress, received feedback, and joined a community of peers on the same journey. The program didn't just remind her—it held her accountable, day by day.

Clinical studies confirmed what her story suggested: participants in Omada's program lost weight, improved glycemic control, and reduced their risk of diabetes progression. The difference wasn't the availability of drugs. It was the reinforcement of behavior.

Propeller Health: Breathing Easier with Data

In Cleveland, a father of two struggled with COPD. Despite prescriptions, he often landed in the ER with flare-ups. His inhaler worked—but only when he used it consistently.

Propeller Health attached a sensor to his inhaler that tracked every puff, linked usage to environmental triggers, and sent him reminders when doses were missed. His physician received adherence reports and adjusted care accordingly. Within months, ER visits dropped. His daily life became less about gasping for air and more about living it.

On a population level, studies have shown that Propeller reduces hospitalizations and improves the quality of life for patients with asthma and COPD. What had once been an invisible problem—adherence—became visible, trackable, and solvable.

Kaia Health: Tackling Chronic Back Pain Anywhere

A 55-year-old factory worker in Germany had lived with chronic back pain for years. Physical therapy helped, but the appointments were difficult to fit into his schedule and became costly over time.

Kaia Health offered an alternative: a digital therapeutic that delivered guided exercises, mindfulness practices, and education via smartphone. Using motion sensors, the app ensured he performed exercises correctly. Over time, his pain lessened, his mobility improved, and his reliance on pain medication decreased.

Trials comparing Kaia to traditional physical therapy found similar pain reduction outcomes—at lower cost and greater accessibility. For patients who might otherwise go untreated, Kaia put therapy in their pockets.

The Lesson

These case studies reveal a pattern. Chronic diseases are less about catastrophic events and more about the cumulative effects of our choices. Digital therapeutics thrive here because they:

- Omada: change behavior one decision at a time.
- Propeller: make adherence visible and actionable.
- Kaia: bring therapy to patients wherever they are.

They succeed not by replacing medicine, but by embedding themselves into the daily fabric of life, where chronic disease is actually managed—or mismanaged.

Closing Thought

What Omada, Propeller, and Kaia demonstrate is that the true frontier of healthcare isn't just in hospitals or clinics—it's in kitchens, workplaces, and commutes. Chronic disease management isn't a battle fought once; it's fought every day.

Digital therapeutics don't just extend the reach of medicine. They change the battlefield entirely—meeting patients in the ordinary moments where extraordinary change happens.

Chapter 3

The Regulatory Landscape for Digital Therapeutics

When Pear Therapeutics submitted reSET® to the FDA in 2017, it wasn't just testing an app. It was a testing question: Can software be medicine?

The answer came in the form of an approval letter. reSET® became the first FDA-authorized prescription digital therapeutic, and in that moment, a line was drawn. Digital health apps, no matter how popular, would never be the same as digital therapeutics. One had convenience. The other now had legitimacy.

Regulation, in this story, is not just bureaucracy—it's the bridge between novelty and medicine.

Regulatory Frameworks Across the Globe

In the U.S., the FDA took the lead, creating pathways for "Software as a Medical Device" (SaMD). Products like Somryst for insomnia and EndeavorRx for ADHD followed reSET through those pathways, proving that code could be scrutinized, validated, and approved like any drug or device.

Europe responded with its own frameworks. The EU's Medical Device Regulation (MDR) became the standard, but it was Germany's DiGA Fast-Track that made headlines. For the first time, certain digital therapeutics could be prescribed by doctors and reimbursed nationally, just like pills. Companies like Kaia Health and HelloBetter seized the opportunity, bringing digital therapeutics (DTx) into the mainstream of healthcare.

Elsewhere, Japan, South Korea, and Singapore began experimenting with their own regulatory approaches, recognizing that the digital therapeutic revolution would be global rather than regional.

The message was clear: software was no longer just technology—it was a form of therapy.

Navigating the Approval Process: From Concept to Market

For start-ups, the approval process can feel like an obstacle course. Unlike wellness apps, which can launch overnight, digital therapeutics must endure years of validation.

Take Somryst®. Built on cognitive behavioral therapy for insomnia, it needed more than good design to succeed. It had to prove the safety, efficacy, and durability of outcomes through randomized controlled trials. Only then did the FDA grant approval, making it the first prescription digital therapeutic (DTx) for sleep disorders.

The irony? While developers often see regulation as a barrier, in practice, it becomes a differentiator. Approval doesn't just open doors to physicians and payers—it signals to the world that this is not a gadget, but a therapy.

Ensuring Compliance: Data Privacy, Security, and Patient Safety

Traditional therapies are evaluated based on their safety and efficacy. Digital therapeutics add another layer: trust in data.

What if a software glitch altered treatment instructions? What if patient data were hacked? What if the algorithm embedded bias? These aren't theoretical risks—they are real, and regulators know it.

That's why frameworks like HIPAA in the U.S. and GDPR in the European Union impose strict requirements on data security, privacy, and transparency. Digital therapeutics must prove they are safe not just clinically, but digitally.

For patients, this means more than legal compliance—it means confidence. A therapy that lives in your pocket must be as secure as it is effective.

Challenges and Opportunities in Regulatory Approval

The path is not easy. Clinical trials are expensive. Approval timelines can stretch for years. For small start-ups, the process can feel existential.

Yet the opportunities are just as great. Regulation elevates quality, weeds out unproven products, and creates trust with physicians, patients, and payers. Germany's DiGA demonstrated how the right framework could accelerate adoption—companies that passed the test gained national reimbursement and mainstream prescribing almost immediately.

For digital therapeutics, regulation is paradoxical: the very scrutiny that slows them down also makes them viable at scale.

Closing Thought

Every revolution needs referees. For digital therapeutics, regulators are not just referees—they are architects. By holding code to the same standards as chemistry, they are rewriting the very definition of medicine.

Without regulation, digital therapeutics would remain clever experiments in app stores. With regulation, they have become therapies capable of standing shoulder to shoulder with drugs and devices.

And that is why the story of digital therapeutics is not just about innovation. It is about legitimacy.

3.1 Regulatory Frameworks Across the Globe: FDA, EMA, and Other Key Markets

When the FDA approved reSET® in 2017, it did more than authorize a single product. It set a precedent: software could now be classified, scrutinized, and sanctioned as a medical device. That decision reverberated across the world, forcing other regulators to ask: if the United States can prescribe code, how should we respond?

The story of digital therapeutics regulation is less about one agency and more about a global patchwork of frameworks—each reflecting different philosophies of healthcare, innovation, and risk.

The United States: The FDA as First Mover

The FDA was the first major regulator to explicitly define and create pathways for Software as a Medical Device (SaMD). Through pilot programs like the Digital Health Software Precertification Program, it began experimenting with how to evaluate software differently from hardware or drugs—focusing on continuous monitoring and updates rather than one-time approvals.

- reSET® (substance use disorder), Somryst® (insomnia), and EndeavorRx® (ADHD) all traveled this path, proving that apps could meet the same gold-standard scrutiny as pharmaceuticals.
- For the FDA, the bigger challenge was cultural: convincing physicians, payers, and patients that what they were prescribing wasn't a gimmick but genuine therapy.

The FDA's leadership gave legitimacy to digital therapeutics and emboldened innovators elsewhere.

Europe: EMA and National Health Authorities

In Europe, regulation is a two-tier system. The European Medicines Agency (EMA) provides broad oversight, but individual nations apply their own frameworks.

Germany emerged as the trailblazer. In 2019, it launched the DiGA Fast-Track program, a groundbreaking initiative that enabled doctors to prescribe approved digital therapeutics and insurers to reimburse them nationwide.

Companies like Kaia Health (for chronic pain) and HelloBetter (for depression and anxiety) became some of the first to be listed in Germany's DiGA directory.

This was more than just regulatory approval—it was market access on a scale. By reimbursing DTx-like drugs, Germany signaled that software had earned a permanent seat in mainstream healthcare.

Other European countries, from France to the Nordics, began observing the German model as a blueprint.

Asia: Innovation Meets Caution

Across Asia, the approach has been diverse.

- **Japan:** Approved the country's first digital therapeutic for nicotine addiction in 2020, reflecting its openness to blending traditional medicine with software-based interventions.
- **South Korea:** Launched pilot programs to integrate digital therapeutics into national health insurance, particularly for mental health and chronic diseases.
- **Singapore:** Positioned itself as a testing ground for innovative health technologies, offering regulatory "sandboxes" where start-ups could trial products under close supervision.
- Here, the emphasis is on balancing innovation with oversight, ensuring that DTx expands access without compromising patient safety.

The Lesson

What emerges from these global efforts is not uniformity but momentum.

- The U.S. has proven that digital therapeutics can be approved.
- Germany demonstrated that it could be prescribed and reimbursed at scale.
- Japan and South Korea demonstrated their ability to adapt to diverse cultural and healthcare system contexts.

Together, these frameworks form a mosaic—a world that is cautiously but steadily converging on the idea that software is not just technology, but also therapy.

Closing Thought

When a doctor in Boston prescribes reSET®, a physician in Berlin prescribes Kaia, and a clinician in Tokyo prescribes a nicotine cessation digital therapeutic (DTx), it signals more than isolated innovation. It signals a global shift. Regulators, once the gatekeepers of drugs and devices, are now becoming the architects of a new therapeutic category.

And with each approval, the question shifts from can software be medicine to how many diseases can software help us treat?

3.2 Navigating the Approval Process: From Concept to Market

When Pear Therapeutics first pitched reSET® to the FDA, they weren't just presenting data—they were presenting a challenge. The agency had reviewed drugs, devices, and biologics for decades. But now it faced something new: an algorithm that claimed to treat disease. How do you regulate therapy that lives in lines of code?

The approval process that followed was long, costly, and painstaking. Yet it created a template: the journey every digital therapeutic must take from idea to prescription.

Step One: Defining the Claim

Every DTx starts with a promise. But regulators want precision: what, exactly, does this software treat?

- Pear defined reSET'®s claim narrowly—substance use disorder, not "wellness" or "habit control."
- Akili Interactive, in contrast, defined EndeavorRx around pediatric ADHD, anchoring the therapeutic mechanism in measurable improvements in attention.

This precision matters. A vague claim sinks a product into the swamp of wellness apps. A specific claim elevates it into medicine.

Step Two: Building the Evidence

Once the claim is defined, evidence becomes the proving ground. And unlike consumer apps, anecdotes and user ratings don't count. Regulators demand randomized controlled trials (RCTs), validated endpoints, and peer-reviewed data.

- Somryst, developed for chronic insomnia, utilizes Cognitive Behavioral Therapy for Insomnia (CBT-I) in a digital format. It ran RCTs showing patients fell asleep faster, woke up less, and maintained results long after completing the program.
- Kaia Health tested its digital therapy for back pain (DTx) against in-person physical therapy and found comparable outcomes at a lower cost.

Each trial not only satisfied regulators—it built trust among physicians and payers.

Step Three: Submitting to Scrutiny

With evidence in hand, the software is now subject to regulatory review. Unlike drugs, which are static once approved, digital therapeutics are dynamic—they can be updated, patched, even redesigned. Regulators have had to rethink their approach, often requiring post-market surveillance and continuous monitoring.

Pear's reSET® became the test case. Its approval forced the FDA to outline expectations for Software as a Medical Device (SaMD), setting precedents for how future products would be evaluated.

Step Four: The Market Reality Check

Approval, however, is not the finish line. It is the entry ticket to the next stage: persuading doctors to prescribe, insurers to reimburse, and patients to engage. This "market reality check" often blindsides developers who assume approval equals adoption.

- Pear had to educate physicians on how to prescribe software.
- Omada Health had to demonstrate to insurers that its diabetes prevention program resulted in reduced long-term costs.
- Akili had to convince parents that a video game could be as legitimate as a pill.

Regulation legitimizes the product. Adoption legitimizes the category.

The Lesson

The approval process for digital therapeutics is not a linear process. It is iterative, demanding clarity of claims, rigor of evidence, transparency in safety, and persistence in adoption.

What makes it different from drug development is not just the raw material (code vs. chemistry), but the rhythm: digital therapeutics evolve, update, and adapt even after approval, requiring regulators, developers, and clinicians to think in cycles, not single endpoints.

Closing Thought

The journey from concept to market is less about persuading regulators that software works and more about proving to the world that therapy can live on a screen.

Pear, Akili, and Kaia show the path: start with a precise claim, back it with clinical data, survive regulatory scrutiny, and then—hardest of all—win adoption in the real world.

In this sense, the approval process is not just a hurdle. It is a rite of passage, transforming ambitious code into trusted medicine.

3.3 Ensuring Compliance: Data Privacy, Security, and Patient Safety

In 2018, a large U.S. health system discovered that a seemingly harmless diabetes-tracking app was quietly sharing user data with third-party advertisers. For patients, the revelation was more than unsettling. Their most intimate health information—their blood sugar logs, daily routines, even emotional notes—was being sold as marketing currency.

This incident underscored a truth regulators already knew: when medicine goes digital, data itself becomes part of the therapy. And with that shift comes a new kind of responsibility.

The New Safety Risks

With drugs, safety is about chemistry: side effects, toxicity, dosage. With digital therapeutics, safety includes something more invisible: software reliability.

- What if a glitch in Somryst® miscalculated a therapy schedule, worsening a patient's insomnia instead of improving it?
- What if a bug in reSET® skipped critical behavioral modules for patients in recovery?
- What if an algorithm in a back pain app like Kaia Health reinforced incorrect movements, leading to injury?

For regulators, these aren't hypothetical concerns. They are part of the approval process. DTx must prove not only clinical efficacy but also algorithmic stability and functional reliability.

The Data Privacy Imperative

A pill doesn't know who you are. A digital therapeutic does. It collects data—sometimes continuously—on symptoms, adherence, habits, and even location. That data, if mishandled, can expose patients to risks beyond health.

This is why regulators lean heavily on frameworks like HIPAA in the U.S. and GDPR in Europe. Developers must prove data is encrypted, anonymized, and secure against breaches. Patients must give informed consent, with clarity on what data is collected and why.

For example, Propeller Health, whose sensors track every inhaler use, had to build compliance safeguards to ensure that inhaler data—linked directly to patients' respiratory health—remains protected from misuse.

The Hidden Risk of Bias

Beyond privacy and glitches lies another subtle risk: algorithmic bias. If a digital therapeutic is trained on narrow patient populations, it may fail—or worse, harm—others.

Imagine a digital therapeutic for depression trained mostly on urban populations, but prescribed in rural areas where cultural expressions of distress differ. Or an ADHD game tested on boys, but prescribed equally to girls, where symptom presentation often diverges.

Regulators are beginning to demand transparency: not just "does it work?" but "for whom does it work?"

Compliance as Trust-Building

For developers, compliance may feel like bureaucracy. But for patients, it is the foundation of trust. A person won't share their most intimate behavioral data with an app unless they believe it is safe, private, and transparent.

This is why Deprexis, a European DTx for depression, placed strong emphasis on secure servers and anonymization protocols. Without them, adoption would have faltered—not because of doubts about efficacy, but because of fears about exposure.

The Lesson

Compliance in digital therapeutics is not just a checklist. It is the difference between skepticism and trust.

- Drugs prove safety in the lab.
- DTx proves safety in the cloud.

Both matter equally to patients.

Closing Thought

The power of digital therapeutics lies in their intimacy—they reside on devices that accompany us, observe us, and respond to us in real-time. But that intimacy is a double-edged sword. It can heal or betray.

By holding DTx to the highest standards of data privacy, security, and patient safety, regulators are not simply policing innovation. They are protecting the fragile trust on which the entire category depends.

Without trust, digital therapeutics are just apps. With trust, they are medicine.

3.4 Challenges and Opportunities in Regulatory Approval

When Pear Therapeutics finally secured FDA approval for reSET®, the celebration inside the company was short-lived. Yes, they had broken ground as the world's first prescription digital therapeutic. But the approval had come after years of costly trials, endless regulatory dialogue, and a level of scrutiny most software companies never face.

Pear's story highlights the paradox at the heart of digital therapeutics regulation: the very system that slows them down is also what makes them legitimate.

The Challenges: Time, Cost, and Complexity

Bringing a wellness app to market can take months. Bringing a digital therapeutic to approval can take years.

- **Time:** Developers must design and run randomized controlled trials, publish results, and respond to regulator feedback—processes that stretch timelines far beyond consumer tech norms.
- **Cost:** These trials and regulatory submissions cost millions, often out of reach for small start-ups without access to venture capital or pharmaceutical partnerships.
- **Complexity:** Unlike drugs, which remain stable once approved, digital therapeutics evolve with updates. Regulators must evaluate not just a snapshot but a living product—creating uncertainty for developers.

For many young companies, these barriers feel existential.

The Opportunities: Legitimacy and Scale

Yet the very barriers that frustrate innovators also create trust. When the FDA or EMA approves a digital therapeutic, it signals to physicians, patients, and insurers that this isn't "just another app." It's therapy.

- Germany's DiGA Fast-Track transformed barriers into an opportunity. By creating a structured approval and reimbursement process for DTx, Germany gave companies like Kaia Health (chronic pain) and HelloBetter (depression, anxiety) national legitimacy. Once listed in the DiGA directory, these DTx were reimbursed by insurers and prescribed by doctors, scaling adoption almost overnight.

- Pear's reSET® and Somryst® in the U.S. gained first-mover credibility. Despite market challenges, those FDA approvals remain benchmarks, giving Pear a reputation as the company that has proven digital therapeutics can be regulated as medicine.

The Tension: Start-Ups vs. Systems

Here lies the tension: start-ups thrive on speed, iteration, and agility. Regulators thrive on caution, data, and stability. Bridging these cultures is difficult.

Some innovators, like Akili Interactive with EndeavorRx, learned to play both games—running rigorous trials while designing an experience that resembles consumer tech. Others faltered, unable to maintain momentum while waiting years for approvals.

But those who endure emerge stronger. Regulation becomes a moat, protecting them from a flood of copycat wellness apps.

The Lesson

The regulatory process for digital therapeutics encompasses more than just safety. It is about the signal. Approval signals to physicians that they can prescribe with confidence, to payers that they can reimburse with justification, and to patients that they can trust what they're using.

The pain of the process is the price of legitimacy.

Closing Thought

The story of digital therapeutics regulation is, in many ways, a story of friction. Start-ups push for speed; regulators pull for safety. The result is a slower, more expensive path than many innovators expect.

But it is precisely that friction that turns ambition into acceptance. Without it, DTx would remain in app stores. With it, they sit in pharmacies.

The challenge is the opportunity: to transform code into cure, innovators must embrace regulation not as an obstacle but as their most powerful ally.

Chapter 4

Developing Digital Therapeutics: A Step-by-Step Guide

When Akili Interactive set out to design EndeavorRx®, the first FDA-approved video game to treat pediatric ADHD, the team didn't start with code. They began with a question: Could a game enhance attention pathways in the brain, just as a pill does in chemistry?

The answer, years later, was yes—but the journey was long, winding, and instructive. It reflected the path that nearly every successful digital therapeutic must take: from identifying unmet needs to designing interventions, building partnerships, generating evidence, securing funding, navigating development cycles, and finally launching at scale.

This is the anatomy of how digital therapeutics are born.

Step One: Identifying Unmet Needs and Patient Pain Points

Every breakthrough begins with empathy. Medicine already has powerful drugs, but too often they fail in practice. Why? Because of behavior, access, or adherence.

- **Diabetes:** Patients take pills but struggle with daily choices. Omada Health identified the gap and developed a program that reinforced habits through coaching, data, and gentle nudges.
- **Depression:** Therapists are scarce in rural areas. Deprexis filled the access gap with digital CBT modules that patients could use anywhere.
- **Substance Use Disorder:** Relapse rates remained high. Pear's reSET® digitized CBT to sustain recovery between clinic visits.

The Lesson

Unmet needs are rarely in the molecule. They are in the patient's lived experience.

Step Two: Designing the Therapeutic Intervention

Identifying the gap is only half the battle. The real challenge is translating therapy into a software solution.

- Somryst® digitized CBT-I for insomnia, carefully adapting 50-minute therapy sessions into short, interactive modules. Clinical rigor met user-friendly design.
- EndeavorRx went further—designing therapy as a form of play. Every spaceship, every challenge, was built to engage children while stimulating neural pathways.

Design in DTx is not cosmetic. Engagement is the mechanism of action. If patients don't use it, it doesn't work.

Step Three: Collaborating with Healthcare Providers and Tech Partners

No digital therapeutic succeeds alone.

- Propeller Health partnered with physicians, ensuring inhaler sensors were seen not as gadgets but as clinical tools.
- Pear Therapeutics partnered with Novartis, gaining access to resources and distribution capabilities.
- Dexcom and Apple have integrated continuous glucose monitoring into the Apple Watch, enabling users to turn data into informed daily decision-making.

Physicians bring trust. Pharma brings scale. Tech platforms bring integration. Together, they transform potential into adoption.

Step Four: Building a Robust Clinical Evidence Base

Without evidence, a DTx is just another app. With evidence, it becomes medicine.

- Somryst® ran RCTs showing durable improvements in sleep.

- Kaia Health demonstrated that its digital therapy for back pain (DTx) was as effective as in-person therapy.
- reSET® demonstrated higher abstinence rates in substance use disorder patients compared to standard care.

In digital therapeutics, trials are not optional—they are the currency of legitimacy.

Step Five: Securing Funding and Strategic Partnerships

Evidence is expensive. Few start-ups can survive without outside support.

- Pear's partnership with Novartis gave it credibility and capital to expand.
- Omada Health secured payer contracts by proving cost savings, ensuring financial viability.
- Happify Health sought pharma alliances to align digital mental health with existing therapeutic portfolios.

Funding provides the runway. Partnerships provide the ecosystem. Together, they turn survival into scale.

Step Six: Navigating the Product Development Lifecycle

Digital therapeutics evolve differently from drugs. They are dynamic, iterative, and often messy.

- Kaia Health pivoted mid-development, adding motion sensors after pilots revealed patients were doing exercises incorrectly.
- Propeller Health refined its design after noticing patients weren't syncing devices consistently.

Unlike a pill, a DTx isn't "done" at approval. It's continuously updated, tested, and improved—demanding agility without compromising safety.

Step Seven: Launching and Scaling Digital Therapeutics

Approval isn't the end. It's the beginning. The challenge is not just launching but persuading an ecosystem to believe.

- Somryst® needed physicians trained to prescribe software.
- Propeller Health needed patients to see inhaler sensors as empowering, not intrusive.

- Germany's DiGA Fast-Track showed how reimbursement systems can accelerate scaling—by listing approved DTx in a national registry, instantly accessible to doctors and covered by insurers.

Scaling requires education, reimbursement, and cultural change. The product may be digital, but adoption is profoundly human.

Closing Thought

From Omada to Kaia, and from reSET to EndeavorRx, the path is remarkably consistent. Empathy sparks the idea. Design translates therapy into code. Partnerships provide reach. Evidence builds trust. Funding fuels growth. Iteration ensures resilience. And scaling turns novelty into normalcy.

The journey is not easy. But when it works, the result is extraordinary: a prescription not written in milligrams or milliliters, but in megabytes.

That is how code becomes cure.

4.1 Identifying Unmet Needs and Patient Pain Points

Every successful therapeutic innovation—digital or otherwise—starts with the same question: Where is medicine failing the patient?

The answer rarely lies in a laboratory. More often, it lies in the lived experience of patients—the late-night struggles, the forgotten pills, the silent relapses that never make it into a doctor's notes. Identifying these unmet needs is less about market research and more about empathy: stepping into the patient's shoes and tracing the invisible cracks where care falls apart.

The Case of Diabetes: Beyond the Pill

Diabetes is one of the most medicated conditions in the world, and yet outcomes remain frustratingly inconsistent. Why? Because the real challenge isn't prescribing metformin—it's helping patients change lifelong habits around food, exercise, and adherence.

Traditional medicine can lower blood sugar in the short term, but it cannot walk with the patient into a bakery on a rainy afternoon when cravings overwhelm discipline. Digital therapeutics step into precisely that moment, offering nudges, real-time monitoring, and personalized coaching. Omada Health, for example, identified this behavioral gap and built a program that combines data tracking with behavioral science—helping patients not only know what to do but actually do it.

Mental Health: The Therapy Desert

In rural Montana, it can take three months to secure an appointment with a licensed therapist. For many patients with depression, that wait can mean worsening symptoms, missed work, or worse. The unmet need here isn't just treatment—it's access.

This is the gap that digital therapeutics like Deprexis sought to fill. By translating cognitive behavioral therapy into digital modules accessible at any time, it provided a lifeline for patients in places where therapists were few and far between. The insight was simple but profound: when geography is the barrier, software can become the bridge.

Substance Use Disorder: The Cycle of Relapse

Substance use disorder presents another type of pain point: relapse rates are stubbornly high, even with medication-assisted therapy. The missing link? Continuous behavioral support. Patients often leave the clinic motivated, only to relapse weeks later in the face of cravings and stressors.

Pear Therapeutics identified this gap and developed reSET®, a digital therapeutic that delivers cognitive behavioral therapy via smartphone. It keeps the patient engaged between appointments, offering structured exercises and reinforcement when willpower alone falters. By embedding therapy into daily life, it addressed a need that no pill could fix.

The Lesson

Unmet needs in healthcare are rarely hidden—they are painfully obvious to both patients and clinicians. The challenge is to recognize them not as inconveniences but as opportunities for intervention.

Diabetes management is not just about glucose levels—it's about behavior. Mental health is not just about treatment—it's about access. Substance use disorder is not just about detox—it's about preventing relapse.

Digital therapeutics succeed when they target these cracks in the system, transforming them from blind spots into entry points for innovation.

4.2 Designing the Therapeutic Intervention: Clinical and Technical Considerations

If identifying unmet needs is about empathy, designing the intervention is about translation—turning medical insight into digital action. It's where the abstract becomes tangible, where the science of therapy collides with the art of design.

The challenge is deceptively simple: How do you take what works in a doctor's office and make it work on a screen?

The Balancing Act: Science Meets Usability

Consider the story of Somryst®, a digital therapeutic for chronic insomnia. Cognitive Behavioral Therapy for Insomnia (CBT-I) has long been the gold standard, but access to trained therapists is limited. The solution seemed obvious: deliver CBT-I digitally.

But here was the catch—what works in a 50-minute face-to-face session doesn't necessarily work on a phone. Clinical rigor demanded fidelity to the CBT-I protocol, while patient usability demanded brevity, interactivity, and engagement. Somryst succeeded because it respected both worlds: clinically validated modules presented in an accessible, user-friendly way that patients could stick with night after night.

This balance—between the uncompromising demands of science and the practicalities of human behavior—is the essence of digital therapeutic design.

Gamification: The Case of ADHD

When Akili Interactive set out to treat pediatric ADHD, they didn't ask: How do we digitize existing therapy? They asked: What would therapy look like if it were designed as a game?

The result, EndeavorRx, resembles a video game—featuring colorful graphics, challenges, and rewards—but every element is carefully engineered to target neural pathways associated with attention. Children play, but the game itself is the therapy. Clinical trials showed measurable improvements in attention span, leading to FDA approval.

This example illustrates a powerful lesson: good design is not an afterthought in digital therapeutics. It is the therapeutic mechanism. Engagement is not cosmetic; it is clinical.

Designing for Diversity: One Size Doesn't Fit All

A digital therapeutic for diabetes in the U.S. cannot simply be "exported" to rural India or urban Japan. Cultural differences, literacy levels, and access to technology shape how interventions must be designed.

Kaia Health, which offers digital physical therapy for back pain, learned this firsthand. Their product had to account for differences in exercise habits, pain perception, and even smartphone use across geographies. The core science remained the same, but the design—language, tone, visuals—shifted to fit patient realities.

Designing a DTx is less about universal templates and more about local translation.

The Lesson

Designing digital therapeutics is not a linear process. It's a negotiation between disciplines:

- Medicine ensures the therapy works.
- Psychology ensures it resonates with human behavior.
- Design ensures it's usable, engaging, and sustainable.

The magic happens when all three align. Too much science without usability, and patients drop off. Too much design without rigor, and regulators reject it. Too much psychology without evidence, and physicians won't prescribe it.

The best digital therapeutics find harmony—like Somryst balancing CBT-I with patient usability, or EndeavorRx blending neuroscience with gamification.

In this sense, designing a DTx is not just engineering. It is storytelling—taking the story of science and writing it in a language the patient can live.

4.3 Collaborating with Healthcare Providers and Tech Partners

If you want to understand why some digital therapeutics succeed while others vanish quietly into app stores, don't just look at the product—look at the partnerships.

A brilliant algorithm can remain unused if physicians don't prescribe it. A beautifully designed app can fail if insurers won't reimburse it. A clinically validated program can stall if patients never hear about it. Success in digital therapeutics isn't just about what you build—it's about who you build it with.

The Physician's Gatekeeping Role

In medicine, trust is currency. Patients rarely adopt a therapy simply because it looks promising on a screen. They adopt it because their physician recommends it.

Propeller Health, which connects inhalers to digital platforms for asthma and COPD, understood this. Instead of marketing directly to patients, they partnered with healthcare providers. Doctors could now track inhaler usage and environmental triggers through dashboards, offering real-time feedback during consultations. The partnership reframed Propeller not as a gadget but as a clinical tool—and adoption soared.

The lesson is simple: without physician buy-in, even the most elegant digital therapeutic risks irrelevance.

Pharma Partnerships: The Muscle of Scale

Pear Therapeutics may have pioneered FDA-approved DTx, but their ambitions outgrew the size of a start-up. To reach scale, they needed partners with deep clinical credibility and market access. Enter Novartis.

The partnership gave Pear more than funding—it gave them a distribution engine, regulatory expertise, and the legitimacy of being associated with one of the world's largest pharmaceutical companies. For Novartis, it opened a new frontier: moving beyond drugs to software-enabled therapies.

This symbiosis is becoming the blueprint. Pharma brings reach and infrastructure; start-ups bring agility and innovation. Together, they accelerate not just development but adoption.

Tech Giants: Infrastructure and Ecosystems

Then there are the tech companies. Apple, Google, and Microsoft are not developing digital therapeutics per se, but their platforms—smartphones, wearables, cloud services—are the stage on which DTx perform.

Take the collaboration between Apple and Dexcom. By integrating continuous glucose monitoring data into Apple Watch, they transformed diabetes management from a clinical task into an everyday glance-at-your-wrist behavior. The therapeutic effect was not in Apple's code or Dexcom's sensor alone—but in their integration.

This shows that tech partners don't just provide tools. They shape the patient's experience of therapy itself.

The Lesson

Collaboration in digital therapeutics is not optional—it is existential.

- Without physicians, there would be no prescriptions.
- Without pharma, there is no scale.
- Without tech, there is no seamless patient experience.

Each partner fills a gap the others cannot. Alone, digital therapeutics risk being "just another app." Together, they become medicine.

Closing Thought

Innovation in healthcare has always been collaborative—vaccines needed labs, logistics, and governments; new drugs needed researchers, regulators, and manufacturers. Digital therapeutics are no different.

But the twist is that in DTx, the partnerships are even more unlikely: a start-up coder, a global pharma executive, a family physician, and a tech giant may all sit at the same table. The result of that unlikely coalition is what turns lines of code into a cure.

4.4 Building a Robust Clinical Evidence Base

In 2016, Pear Therapeutics was on the cusp of history. They had developed reSET®, a software program for substance use disorder. It looked promising, but in medicine, "promising" means nothing without proof.

So they did something bold: they put their code through the same gauntlet as a drug. Randomized controlled trials. Peer-reviewed publications. Measurable endpoints. The results were clear—patients using reSET were significantly more likely to stay abstinent than those who didn't. And in 2017, the FDA approved reSET as the world's first prescription digital therapeutic.

That moment underscored a truth that every DTx developer eventually faces: clinical evidence isn't just paperwork. It is the passport that turns an app into medicine.

Why Evidence Matters?

A wellness app can thrive on user reviews and downloads. "It made me feel better" is enough for consumers. However, digital therapeutics aim to sit alongside drugs in a physician's toolkit. That means they must speak the language of medicine: randomized controlled trials (RCTs), validated endpoints, safety monitoring, and long-term follow-up.

Without evidence, DTx are just gadgets. With evidence, they become therapies.

Case Study 1: Somryst and Insomnia

Cognitive Behavioral Therapy for Insomnia (CBT-I) is highly effective, but access to trained therapists is limited. Somryst digitized CBT-I, but they didn't stop at design. They ran rigorous clinical trials.

In one landmark study, patients using Somryst reported falling asleep faster, waking less at night, and maintaining improvements months later. That evidence convinced the FDA, making Somryst the first prescription digital therapeutic for insomnia.

The clinical data didn't just prove efficacy. It reassured physicians that they could prescribe it with confidence, and payers that they could reimburse it with justification.

Case Study 2: Kaia Health and Back Pain

Back pain is one of the leading causes of disability worldwide. Kaia Health has built a digital therapeutics (DTx) platform that delivers personalized physical therapy and mindfulness exercises via smartphone. But they knew that in a crowded wellness market, evidence would be their differentiator.

Clinical trials compared Kaia's app to in-person physical therapy. The result? Comparable improvements in pain reduction—at a fraction of the cost and with greater accessibility. By publishing peer-reviewed results, Kaia moved from "interesting app" to "validated therapy."

Case Study 3: reSET and Substance Use Disorder

Pear's reSET showed how digital therapeutics can transform outcomes in complex conditions. In RCTs, patients using reSET alongside standard care achieved higher abstinence rates and better treatment retention than those receiving standard care alone.

The evidence not only won FDA approval but also opened reimbursement pathways, since payers could see the economic value of reduced relapses and hospital visits.

The Lesson

Building a clinical evidence base is not optional in digital therapeutics. It is the difference between being downloaded and being prescribed. Between being a gadget and being reimbursed. Between being a novelty and being a necessity.

Every successful DTx carries a story of proof: Somryst showing long-term sleep improvements, Kaia proving digital therapy can rival in-person care, Pear demonstrating behavioral outcomes through code.

The thread tying these stories together is trust. In medicine, evidence is how trust is built. And in digital therapeutics, trust is everything.

Closing Thought

A digital therapeutic without evidence is like a drug without trials—an idea without credibility. But when evidence is strong, something remarkable happens: the code is no longer just code. It becomes a prescription, a therapy, a legitimate part of modern medicine.

This is how digital therapeutics earn their seat at the clinical table—not through promise, but through proof.

4.5 Securing Funding and Strategic Partnerships

In 2014, Pear Therapeutics had the science. They had early clinical data suggesting that software could treat substance use disorder. But science, on its own, doesn't pay for randomized trials, regulatory submissions, or physician education. What they lacked was the fuel to keep going—funding.

Enter Novartis. When the pharmaceutical giant partnered with Pear, it wasn't just writing a check. It was signaling something more powerful: that digital therapeutics had crossed from a start-up curiosity into the serious business of medicine. With Novartis 'backing, Pear scaled trials, navigated regulatory pathways, and built the infrastructure needed to launch reSET®.

This was the moment many in healthcare realized that digital therapeutics weren't just apps with ambition. They were therapies with investors, allies, and a future.

Why Funding Matters in DTx

Drug development is famously expensive. But digital therapeutics, while leaner, still require significant capital. Clinical trials, regulatory approval, software development, data security, payer negotiations—all demand resources.

Unlike consumer apps, which can thrive on venture capital and viral growth, DTx companies must spend years building evidence before generating revenue. Without patient capital—or strategic partnerships—they risk running out of runway before reaching the market.

Funding isn't just money. It's time, survival, and legitimacy.

Strategic Partnerships: More than Capital

Money alone doesn't guarantee success. What distinguishes the winners in DTx is who stands beside them.

- **Pharma as Partner:** When Sanofi partnered with Happify Health to explore digital therapeutics for depression and anxiety, it wasn't just about investing in software. It was about aligning with a therapeutic area Sanofi already knew deeply, creating synergy between pills and pixels.
- **Insurers as Allies:** Omada Health understood that for digital prevention programs to succeed, payers had to be on board. By demonstrating

reduced long-term costs in diabetes prevention, they secured reimbursement contracts with major insurers—turning their product from a consumer app into a reimbursable therapy.

- **Tech Platforms as Enablers:** Kaia Health's partnership with Apple's ecosystem allowed seamless integration of physical therapy exercises into devices patients already used daily. This wasn't just convenience—it was adoption at scale.

These partnerships provide distribution channels, regulatory expertise, patient access, and—perhaps most importantly—trust.

The Risks of Going it Alone

Digital therapeutics built in isolation often falter. Start-ups that underestimate the complexity of healthcare systems—thinking a slick app and some pilot data will suffice—find themselves ignored by physicians, unsupported by payers, and starved of cash.

The lesson is stark: in healthcare, success isn't just about innovation. It's about integration.

Case Study: Pear and Novartis

Pear's partnership with Novartis remains a defining case. For Novartis, it was an entry into the digital frontier. For Pear, it was survival and scale. However, the alliance also revealed tensions—cultural differences between agile start-ups and established pharmaceutical giants. Eventually, Pear charted its own course, but not before proving that these alliances can elevate a digital therapeutic from obscurity to market leadership.

The Lesson

Funding keeps the lights on. Partnerships open the doors. Together, they transform potential into presence.

In digital therapeutics, the science may win the headlines, but it is capital and collaboration that determine who survives the marathon.

Closing Thought

Every digital therapeutic begins as an idea scribbled on a whiteboard. But turning that idea into a prescribed, reimbursed therapy takes far more than ingenuity. It takes allies—pharma companies willing to share credibility, insurers willing to share risk, and investors willing to share vision.

Without them, even the most brilliant code risks disappearing into the graveyard of forgotten apps. With them, code becomes cure.

4.6 Navigating the Product Development Lifecycle

Every digital therapeutic begins with optimism. The pitch decks are polished, the prototype looks slick, and the vision feels unstoppable. But between that first idea and a therapy doctors can prescribe lies a gauntlet—a product development lifecycle that is as unforgiving as it is essential.

Unlike consumer apps, where "move fast and break things" is a badge of honor, in healthcare, the motto is closer to "move carefully and prove everything." This tension—between agility and rigor—is what defines the digital therapeutics (DTx) journey.

From Prototype to Pilot

Take Kaia Health, which set out to digitize physical therapy for chronic back pain. Their first version was simple: guided exercises on a phone. However, in pilot studies, they found that patients struggled with form—movements weren't always correct, which risked both outcomes and safety.

So they pivoted, adding computer vision to monitor posture in real time. What began as a straightforward app became a far more sophisticated therapeutic tool. The pivot didn't just improve outcomes—it saved the product from irrelevance.

This is the rhythm of DTx development: build, test, learn, refine. Unlike pills, which emerge fully formed after years of lab work, digital therapeutics evolve visibly, shaped by feedback loops.

The Tug-of-War: Speed vs. Evidence

Start-ups often face a brutal trade-off: release quickly to gain traction, or wait until the evidence is bulletproof?

Consider Happify Health, which developed digital interventions for depression and anxiety. Early pilots showed promise, but insurers demanded large-scale clinical data before reimbursement. Patients wanted access now. Regulators wanted rigor. Balancing these demands required a phased strategy—launching pilots to gather real-world evidence while simultaneously running controlled trials.

It's a dance: move too slowly, and you lose momentum. Move too quickly, and you lose credibility.

Scaling the Mountain of Regulation

The regulatory review process often feels like climbing Everest. Each step—pre-submission meetings, trial design approvals, safety audits—adds months, sometimes years.

But companies that survive emerge stronger. Pear Therapeutics, for example, spent years navigating FDA pathways for reSET and Somryst. The result? First-mover advantage and credibility that competitors without approvals could never match.

The lifecycle isn't just about product maturation. It's about earning legitimacy, one regulatory milestone at a time.

Iterating in the Real World

Even after approval, the work doesn't stop. Post-market surveillance, real-world evidence collection, and patient feedback often trigger further refinements.

Propeller Health discovered that patients weren't consistently syncing their inhalers. Instead of blaming users, they redesigned the experience by simplifying sync processes, adding reminders, and refining the app design. The outcome: improved adherence and higher engagement.

This continuous improvement loop is the defining feature of DTx. The therapy doesn't just get launched; it gets lived into existence.

The Lesson

The DTx lifecycle is not linear. It is cyclical: prototype → pilot → clinical trial → regulatory approval → launch → real-world iteration. Each cycle demands humility—the willingness to adapt, refine, and sometimes start over.

Where drugs are static once approved, digital therapeutics are dynamic. They are never "finished." And that adaptability is both their greatest challenge and their greatest strength.

Closing Thought

When we look at success stories like Kaia, Pear, or Propeller, it's tempting to focus on the end product. But their real achievement lies in resilience—the ability to navigate setbacks, embrace pivots, and learn from each stage of development.

The lifecycle of digital therapeutics isn't just about building software. It's about building trust—step by step, cycle by cycle, until what began as code becomes a therapy patients, physicians, and payers believe in.

4.7 Launching and Scaling Digital Therapeutics

When Pear Therapeutics won FDA approval for reSET®, the hard part wasn't over—it was just beginning. They had climbed the mountain of evidence and regulation, only to find another mountain on the horizon: getting doctors to prescribe it, insurers to reimburse it, and patients to use it.

In digital therapeutics, launch isn't a finish line. It's the starting gun for a new kind of race—the race to scale.

The Adoption Puzzle

Launching a digital therapeutic is unlike launching a new app or a new drug. With apps, you need downloads. With drugs, you need prescriptions. With DTx, you need both—and more.

Doctors must be convinced it works. Patients must be willing to engage. Insurers must see economic value. Regulators must be reassured the therapy remains safe as it scales. Each stakeholder represents a gate, and each gate must be unlocked in sequence.

Take Somryst, the prescription digital therapeutic for insomnia. The clinical data was strong. But adoption required more: educating physicians on how to prescribe software, convincing patients that sleep therapy could come through a phone, and ensuring insurers would cover it. Launch wasn't just a marketing campaign. It was a cultural shift.

Building Belief: Physicians and Patients

For physicians, digital therapeutics are still a new terrain. They're trained to prescribe drugs, not downloads. Many hesitate—not because they doubt the science, but because the prescribing process is unfamiliar.

This is where education becomes central. Propeller Health succeeded not only because of its technology but because it invested in showing doctors how the platform fit into asthma and COPD management. By framing Propeller as a clinical tool that augmented their care, it earned their trust.

Patients, meanwhile, must overcome skepticism. A pill feels like medicine. An app? Less so. That's why companies like Kaia Health leaned heavily on testimonials and user stories—helping patients see themselves in the experience, and trust that digital therapy wasn't "less" medicine but a new form of it.

The Reimbursement Barrier

Even the best evidence means little without reimbursement. Patients won't pay out-of-pocket for long-term therapies, and physicians won't prescribe them without insurance coverage.

Germany cracked this problem with its DiGA Fast-Track system, where approved DTx can be listed in a national registry, reimbursed by insurers, and prescribed by doctors. This gave companies like Kaia and HelloBetter a scalable pathway.

In the U.S., reimbursement is still patchier, but pioneers like Omada Health broke through by proving cost savings to insurers. Their diabetes prevention program showed measurable reductions in future healthcare costs—a value proposition insurers couldn't ignore.

Scaling Beyond the First Launch

Launching a digital therapeutic is one thing. Scaling it across populations, conditions, and geographies is another. Cultural differences, regulatory variations, and technology infrastructure all complicate growth.

Kaia Health had to adapt its product design and language for different markets. Pear struggled to align with shifting U.S. reimbursement policies. Omada found that integrating with employer wellness programs created faster adoption than targeting consumers directly.

Scaling, in short, isn't about one big push. It's about adapting, market by market, system by system.

The Lesson

In digital therapeutics, the product is only half the battle. The other half is creating belief—among doctors, patients, and payers. Evidence may get you approval. However, trust, education, and reimbursement drive adoption.

Scaling is not solely a matter of technology. It is a matter of systems, incentives, and human psychology.

Closing Thought

When we think of breakthroughs in medicine, we often picture the moment of discovery: the first insulin injection, the first antibiotic, the first vaccine. But the real story of impact comes later—when those discoveries reach millions.

Digital therapeutics are no different. The launch is not the triumph. The triumph is when thousands of doctors prescribe them, millions of patients use them, and entire healthcare systems embrace them.

That's when code truly becomes cure.

Chapter 5

The Role of Pharma in Digital Therapeutics

For decades, pharmaceutical companies defined therapy by its chemical composition. A blockbuster drug was measured in patents, prescriptions, and profits. So when the first digital therapeutics appeared, pharma's initial response was polite curiosity at best—and quiet skepticism at worst.

But something changed. As reSET®, Somryst®, and EndeavorRx® began winning regulatory approval, the pharmaceutical industry realized that DTx weren't gadgets on the fringe. They were therapies competing for the same patients, the same prescribers, and eventually, the same reimbursement streams. The question for pharma shifted from "Are digital therapeutics real?" to "What role should we play?"

Why Pharma Companies should Invest in Digital Therapeutics ?

The rationale is simple: digital therapeutics address the blind spots of medicine.

- Adherence: Billions are lost every year because patients don't take drugs correctly. A DTx can reinforce reminders, education, and behavioral nudges.
- Differentiation: In crowded therapeutic areas, such as diabetes or depression, adding a digital layer to a pill can set a brand apart.
- Value-based healthcare: Payers want proof of real-world outcomes. DTx generates the kind of continuous data that makes value visible.

Pharma realized that digital therapeutics weren't competition—they were companions. And in a world where outcomes matter as much as molecules, that partnership is powerful.

Strategic Considerations for Pharma: Aligning DTx with Brand Strategy

But investment alone isn't enough. Pharma must align digital therapeutics (DTx) with brand goals.

- A diabetes franchise might integrate a behavioral coaching app, such as Omada Health, to complement insulin therapy.
- An oncology portfolio might explore DTx that support patient adherence to complex chemotherapy regimens.
- A mental health brand might bundle medication with access to Deprexis, creating a holistic treatment package.

The strategy is not "digital for digital's sake," but digital that amplifies existing assets and reinforces brand value.

Partnering with Digital Health Startups: Opportunities and Pitfalls

Pharma rarely builds DTx from scratch. Instead, it partners with startups. But those partnerships come with both promise and pitfalls.

- **Promise:** When Novartis partnered with Pear Therapeutics, it provided Pear with the capital and distribution muscle to scale reSET. In return, Novartis positioned itself as a pioneer.
- **Pitfalls:** Culture clashes are common. Startups thrive on agility, whereas pharma operates under regulation and hierarchy. Misaligned expectations can stall progress—as Pear and Novartis eventually discovered when their partnership fizzled.

The opportunity is clear: pharma brings scale, startups bring innovation. But success depends on mutual trust, shared goals, and cultural fluency.

Commercializing Digital Therapeutics: Market Access and Reimbursement Strategies

Commercializing a digital therapeutic (DTx) differs from commercializing a pill. The barriers are distinct, and the pharmaceutical industry is uniquely positioned to address them.

- **Physician education:** Doctors must learn how to prescribe software. Pharma's salesforces are already trained to bridge knowledge gaps.
- **Payer negotiations:** Insurers need proof of value. Pharma's long-standing payer relationships make it easier to integrate digital therapeutics (DTx) into reimbursement systems.
- **Distribution channels:** Pharma's infrastructure—from medical science liaisons to patient support programs—offers a ready-made launchpad.

This is why Sanofi's collaboration with Happify Health in digital mental health made sense. Sanofi could leverage its commercial muscle, while Happify provided the innovation.

Case Studies: Pharma Companies Leading the Way

Several pharma companies have already stepped into this space:

- Novartis + Pear Therapeutics: Brought the first FDA-approved DTx to scale, proving pharma could be a co-creator.
- Sanofi + Happify Health: Partnered on digital therapeutics for depression and anxiety, aligning with Sanofi's mental health focus.
- Boehringer Ingelheim: Explored DTx for schizophrenia and mental health, leveraging digital to address adherence and access.
- Roche: Invested in DTx solutions for multiple sclerosis, integrating digital monitoring with drug regimens.

Each case signals the same pattern: pharma is no longer a bystander. It is shaping the future of digital therapeutics.

Closing Thought

For a century, the pharmaceutical industry has been defined by pills and patents. But the definition of medicine is expanding. Today, therapy might be a molecule, a device, or an algorithm—and often all three together.

Pharma's role in digital therapeutics is not to replace its legacy, but to extend it: combining the chemistry of yesterday with the code of tomorrow.

Ultimately, the companies that thrive won't be the ones that view DTx as a threat. They'll be the ones that see them for what they really are: the missing piece of the therapeutic puzzle.

5.1 Why Pharma Companies Should Invest in Digital Therapeutics

When Novartis partnered with Pear Therapeutics in 2018, the pharmaceutical world raised its eyebrows. Novartis had blockbuster drugs in oncology and cardiology—what business did it have with a start-up writing code for addiction therapy?

The answer was simple: outcomes.

For decades, the pharmaceutical industry has thrived on molecules. But molecules alone often fail to deliver the outcomes that matter most—not because they're ineffective, but because patients don't take them properly, don't have access to complementary therapies, or don't receive enough behavioral support. Digital therapeutics (DTx) offer a way to close that gap. For pharma, they're not a side project. They're a strategic necessity.

Adherence: The Billion-Dollar Blind Spot

Every pharma executive knows the number: about 50% of patients don't take their medications as prescribed. For chronic diseases, this means lost sales, wasted drugs, and—most importantly—worsened patient outcomes.

- Propeller Health showed how this could be fixed. By attaching sensors to inhalers for asthma and COPD, it tracked adherence in real-time, sent reminders, and provided doctors with actionable data. Patients used their inhalers more consistently. Exacerbations dropped. For a pharma company with a respiratory portfolio, Propeller's model isn't a gadget—it's a sales multiplier and a patient outcome enhancer rolled into one.

Differentiation in Crowded Markets

In therapeutic areas like diabetes or depression, where multiple drugs compete, differentiation is tough. Most pills promise similar efficacy; the battle is won in perception and added value.

- Sanofi's partnership with Happify Health is a prime example. By pairing traditional mental health treatments with digital therapeutics that deliver CBT-based exercises for depression and anxiety, Sanofi added a new layer of value to its portfolio. The drug treats the biology, the DTx addresses the behavior. Together, they stand out in a crowded market.

Generating Real-World Evidence

Healthcare is shifting toward value-based care, where reimbursement is based on demonstrated outcomes. Pharma companies need data—not just from clinical trials, but from the everyday lives of patients.

- Omada Health's diabetes prevention program provided exactly that. By tracking weight, activity, and glucose levels in real-time, it demonstrated reductions in long-term healthcare costs. For pharmaceutical companies in the metabolic disease space, partnering with programs like Omada isn't just about achieving better outcomes—it's about generating a stream of real-world evidence that strengthens reimbursement negotiations.

The Strategic Imperative

Pharma companies don't invest in DTx because they want to be in the app business. They invest because:

- DTx enhances adherence, which in turn improves both patient outcomes and drug revenue.
- DTx creates differentiation, making their therapies more competitive.
- DTx generates data, which is the new currency in value-based healthcare.

The logic is compelling: if the pill works in the lab but fails in real-life applications, the pharmaceutical company loses. If the pill works in life—thanks to a digital companion—everyone wins: the patient, the payer, and the company.

Closing Thought

When Novartis shook hands with Pear, it wasn't just dabbling in technology. It was hedging the future of the pharmaceutical industry itself. Because the companies that embrace digital therapeutics aren't just adding a shiny new tool to their arsenal. They're redefining what it means to deliver therapy in the first place.

The truth is clear: in the years ahead, the most successful pharma companies won't sell drugs alone. They'll sell outcomes—and digital therapeutics are the bridge that makes those outcomes possible.

5.2 Strategic Considerations for Pharma: Aligning Digital Therapeutics with Brand Strategy

When Sanofi began exploring digital mental health, it didn't start by asking, What's the hottest technology out there? Instead, it asked a different question: How do digital therapeutics fit into our portfolio?

This shift—from chasing trends to aligning strategy—is what separates pharma companies that succeed in digital therapeutics from those that don't. Digital tools can be shiny distractions unless they reinforce a brand's therapeutic identity, extend its reach, or strengthen its value proposition.

From Pills to Ecosystems

For decades, the pharmaceutical industry thought in terms of brands as molecules—each drug stood on its own, competing against rivals in its class. But digital therapeutics push companies to think in terms of brands as ecosystems. A pill may address biology, but the ecosystem around it—support, adherence, behavior—can determine whether the brand thrives or fails.

- **Diabetes:** Companies that manufacture insulin or oral hypoglycemics are increasingly seeing digital companions as a strategic asset. Partnering with programs like Omada Health, which utilizes coaching and data to reinforce healthy behaviors, enables a pharma company's brand to be viewed not just as a "drug" but as part of a comprehensive diabetes solution.

Therapy Bundles: Complementing the Molecule

In crowded therapeutic markets, differentiation is everything. Adding a DTx to a brand can transform it from a pill into a therapy package.

- **Mental Health:** Antidepressants often stabilize neurochemistry, but outcomes depend heavily on behavioral reinforcement. By aligning with digital therapeutics like Deprexis or Happify Health, a pharma company can offer prescribers a two-in-one solution: medication plus digital CBT. This makes the brand more attractive to physicians and more effective for patients.

The drug treats biology. The DTx treats behavior. Together, they create a holistic treatment strategy.

The Value-Based Care Advantage

Payers increasingly demand proof of outcomes, not just claims of efficacy. Digital therapeutics generate real-world data that can strengthen a pharma brand's case for reimbursement.

- **Respiratory Care:** A company marketing an inhaler for asthma or COPD might align with Propeller Health. The sensors track adherence and outcomes in real time, creating evidence to support payer negotiations. The message becomes: our brand doesn't just work in trials—it works in life.

Choosing Wisely: Avoiding the Digital Distraction

Not every brand needs a digital companion. A highly curative oncology drug, for example, may derive little incremental value from a digital therapeutic (DTx). Strategic alignment means asking:

- Does this therapeutic area involve long-term adherence or behavior change?
- Can a DTx create measurable value for patients, payers, and providers?
- Does this fit with the company's brand positioning and future roadmap?

Chasing "digital" for its own sake is a recipe for wasted investment. Aligning digital with brand strategy is the difference between novelty and necessity.

Closing Thought

The strategic question for pharma isn't whether we should invest in digital therapeutics. It's where do digital therapeutics amplify our brand story?

When thoughtfully aligned, a pill becomes more than a pill—it becomes part of an ecosystem of care. And in a world moving toward outcomes and value-based contracts, that alignment isn't optional. It's survival.

Pharma brands that recognize this will not just compete. They'll lead.

5.3 Partnering with Digital Health Startups: Opportunities and Pitfalls

When Novartis announced its partnership with Pear Therapeutics in 2018, the pharma world saw it as a bold experiment. A century-old drug giant was betting on a start-up whose flagship product wasn't a pill but a software program for substance use disorder. For a moment, it seemed like the perfect marriage: Novartis would bring credibility, distribution, and market access; Pear would bring agility, innovation, and vision.

And yet, within a few years, the partnership quietly dissolved. The story wasn't about failure as much as it was about friction—the cultural, strategic, and operational differences that can make these collaborations both high-reward and high-risk.

The Opportunity: Scale Meets Innovation

Pharma companies have scale. Start-ups have ideas. Combine them, and the potential is enormous.

- **Pear + Novartis:** Pear had FDA-approved products (reSET®, Somryst) but needed a robust distribution network. Novartis saw a chance to redefine its value proposition—not just selling pills, but selling outcomes. The partnership gave Pear credibility and gave Novartis a foothold in the digital frontier.
- **Sanofi + Happify Health:** Sanofi recognized that Happify's digital CBT platform could enrich its mental health offerings. The collaboration expanded Sanofi's portfolio and positioned Happify as a clinically validated partner rather than just another wellness app.

The opportunity is clear: Start-ups gain funding, regulatory expertise, and sales infrastructure; pharma gains innovation, differentiation, and relevance in a digital-first future.

The Pitfalls: Culture Clashes and Misalignment

But partnerships are rarely seamless. Start-ups and pharma companies are wired differently.

- **Speed vs. Process:** Start-ups thrive on agility—"fail fast, iterate fast." Pharma thrives on regulation, caution, and multi-year timelines. When Pear expected rapid integration and Novartis expected careful, methodical rollout, timelines clashed.
- **Focus vs. Breadth:** Start-ups often bet everything on one product. Pharma spreads resources across entire pipelines. When strategic priorities diverge, commitment wavers.
- **Control vs. Collaboration:** Pharma companies are used to controlling development, branding, and market entry. Start-ups often resist being subsumed into a corporate machine. The friction can stall innovation.

The result? Partnerships collapse not because the science fails, but because the collaboration model cracks.

Learning from Both Sides

Some collaborations, however, demonstrate how the balance can be effective.

- **Propeller Health + AstraZeneca / Novartis:** Propeller partnered with multiple pharma companies to integrate inhaler sensors into respiratory portfolios. The alignment was natural: pharma sold the inhalers, Propeller made them smarter. Both sides won.
- **Kaia Health + European Health Systems:** Kaia developed digital back pain therapy and then partnered with insurers and pharmaceutical companies to scale its distribution. The success came from clarity: Kaia owned the innovation, partners owned the scaling.

The common denominator in successful partnerships is alignment of incentives. When both sides see clear value—better outcomes for patients, better differentiation for pharma, better scale for start-ups—the collaboration endures.

The Lesson

Partnerships between pharma and digital health start-ups are like arranged marriages: they look perfect on paper, but success depends on chemistry.

- **The opportunity:** Pharma gains innovation, start-ups gain scale.
- **The pitfalls:** Mismatched cultures, diverging priorities, power struggles.

- **The solution:** Clarity of goals, patience with process, and shared ownership of outcomes.

Closing Thought

Pharma doesn't need to reinvent itself as a start-up. And start-ups don't need to become pharma-lite. The real magic happens when each side does what it does best—and respects the other for the value it brings.

Ultimately, the question isn't whether pharma and digital start-ups should collaborate. It's how well they can learn to live together.

5.4 Commercializing Digital Therapeutics: Market Access and Reimbursement Strategies

When Somryst®, the FDA-approved digital therapeutic for insomnia, launched, the science was unquestionable. Randomized controlled trials have proven their efficacy. Regulators had given their blessing. Yet adoption lagged. Doctors were intrigued, patients were curious, but insurers were hesitant. The problem wasn't science—it was economics.

In healthcare, no therapy succeeds unless it can navigate the narrow gateways of market access and reimbursement. For digital therapeutics, this hurdle is as critical as regulatory approval. Without reimbursement, patients pay out of pocket; without payer buy-in, physicians hesitate to prescribe. The challenge, then, is not just to prove whether it works, but to prove it is worth paying for.

Educating Physicians: The First Gate

Physicians are the primary gateway to adoption, but many are still unsure how to prescribe software. Unlike a pill, which has well-worn protocols, a digital therapeutic requires explanation: How does the patient access it? What does the prescription look like? How do results get reported back?

- Propeller Health addressed this by integrating its inhaler sensors into the workflows that physicians already used. Instead of positioning itself as "new tech," Propeller framed itself as a clinical tool—a data dashboard doctors could use in consultations. The result? Physicians saw immediate utility, which eased adoption.

Pharma companies, with their vast networks of medical liaisons and sales representatives, are uniquely positioned to bridge this gap—educating doctors, smoothing integration, and making digital therapeutics feel familiar rather than foreign.

Convincing Payers: The Economics of Value

For payers, the equation is simple: a therapy is worth covering if it reduces overall healthcare costs. Digital therapeutics must therefore demonstrate not just clinical efficacy but economic impact.

- Omada Health succeeded by showing that its diabetes prevention program reduced long-term costs for insurers by lowering the incidence of Type 2 diabetes. That financial story—not just the clinical data—secured Omada contracts with major U.S. insurers.
- In Germany, the DiGA Fast-Track has created a national reimbursement pathway for digital therapeutic (DTx). Once products like Kaia Health (for back pain) and HelloBetter (for depression and anxiety) were listed, insurers automatically covered them. This structural alignment transformed adoption almost overnight.

Pharma companies know this playbook. They've spent decades negotiating with payers and defending the value of high-cost therapies. Extending that muscle to digital therapeutics is less a reinvention than an adaptation.

Distribution and Scalability: The Pharma Advantage

Even with payer approval, the scale requires distribution. Small start-ups often lack the infrastructure to reach thousands of physicians or millions of patients. Pharma excels here.

- Sanofi's partnership with Happify Health illustrates the model. Happify brought digital CBT innovation, while Sanofi provided the global sales, distribution, and payer relationships needed to make commercialization viable. The synergy was simple: the start-up created, pharma scaled.

The Lesson

Commercializing a digital therapeutic is not a linear process. It requires passing through multiple gates:

1. Physician adoption, where pharma's educational infrastructure matters.
2. Payer reimbursement, where evidence of cost savings becomes the argument.
3. Distribution at scale, where pharma's reach turns niche tools into mainstream therapies.

The brilliance of the product is necessary but not sufficient. Without market access and reimbursement, even the most effective DTx risks becoming another forgotten app.

Closing Thought

Digital therapeutics promise to transform care, but only if they can survive the harsh economics of healthcare. Science earns approval; economics earns adoption.

This is where pharma's role becomes indispensable. Pharma knows how to navigate insurers, educate physicians, and build effective distribution systems. Start-ups may build the code, but pharma builds the market.

And in that partnership lies the real potential of digital therapeutics—not just to be approved, but to be prescribed, reimbursed, and embraced at scale.

5.5 Case Studies: Pharma Companies Leading the Way in Digital Therapeutics

When digital therapeutics first appeared, most pharmaceutical companies stood on the sidelines. They watched, curious yet cautious, unsure whether software could truly serve as a complementary medicine alongside drugs. But a handful of bold players leaned in early, and their experiments have shaped the playbook for how pharma can lead in this new frontier.

Novartis and Pear Therapeutics: The First Bold Bet

In 2018, Novartis stunned the industry by partnering with Pear Therapeutics, the start-up behind reSET® for substance use disorder and Somryst® for insomnia. For Novartis, this was more than an investment—it was a strategic statement: that pharma's future wasn't confined to molecules.

The partnership gave Pear access to Novartis's regulatory expertise and distribution channels, while Novartis gained credibility as a pioneer. Together, they sought to commercialize Pear's FDA-approved DTx globally.

The partnership eventually ended, a reminder of how cultural and strategic friction can derail collaboration. But its legacy was lasting: Novartis proved that pharma could step into digital therapeutics not as an observer, but as a co-creator.

Sanofi and Happify Health: Mental Health Meets Digital Scale

Sanofi, with a portfolio that touched mental health, saw an opportunity in the growing demand for accessible therapy. It partnered with Happify Health, a digital platform offering CBT-based programs for depression and anxiety.

The logic was straightforward: antidepressants treat neurochemistry, but outcomes improve when paired with behavioral reinforcement. Happify provided the behavioral layer, while Sanofi provided the reach. The partnership positioned Sanofi not only as a drugmaker but also as a holistic mental health company—a move that resonated with payers seeking value-based solutions.

Roche and Multiple Sclerosis: Data as Therapy

Roche, a leader in neuroscience and immunology, uniquely approached digital therapeutics. Instead of a direct app-based therapy, it invested in digital platforms for multiple sclerosis (MS). These tools tracked symptoms, patient-reported outcomes, and disease progression, generating continuous data streams that enhanced care and informed treatment decisions.

For Roche, the opportunity wasn't just in supplementing therapy—it was in integrating digital monitoring with its MS drugs, creating a feedback loop between patient experience and therapeutic strategy.

This data-driven model illustrates how pharma can use digital therapeutics not just to complement drugs, but to redefine care pathways entirely.

Propeller Health and Pharma Partnerships: Inhalers Made Smarter

Propeller Health didn't align with just one pharma company—it partnered with several, including AstraZeneca and Novartis, to integrate digital inhaler sensors into respiratory portfolios.

The result was elegant: the drug remained the same, but Propeller made it smarter. By tracking adherence and environmental triggers, Propeller generated data that improved outcomes and provided pharma with real-world evidence to support reimbursement.

This case demonstrated that pharma doesn't always need to build or own the digital layer—it can partner to enhance existing products and differentiate itself in competitive markets.

The Lesson

These case studies reveal different models of leadership:

- **Novartis + Pear:** Co-creation through bold partnerships.
- **Sanofi + Happify:** Extending drug portfolios with behavioral companions.
- **Roche in MS:** Leveraging digital monitoring as a therapeutic complement.
- **Propeller + pharma partners:** Enhancing existing drugs with digital layers.

Each path is unique, but the common thread is this: pharma no longer sees digital therapeutics as peripheral. It sees them as essential.

Closing Thought

When Novartis, Sanofi, Roche, and AstraZeneca stepped into digital therapeutics, they weren't just experimenting with apps. They were rewriting the definition of what it means to be a pharmaceutical company.

Not just makers of pills. Not just sellers of molecules. But stewards of outcomes—where drugs and digital work together to deliver health in a way neither could achieve alone.

Chapter 6

The Impact of AI and Emerging Technologies on Digital Therapeutics

In 2015, a young boy with Type 1 diabetes strapped on a continuous glucose monitor for the first time. Within days, his parents noticed something remarkable. His phone began buzzing with alerts not just when his blood sugar levels went too high or too low, but also when it predicted they would. For the first time, they weren't reacting to crises—they were preventing them.

That moment captures the quiet revolution AI and emerging technologies are bringing to digital therapeutics. It is not about replacing what already exists, but about making therapy smarter, faster, and more personal.

When you open Spotify, it doesn't just give you music—it gives you your music. A playlist built from your listening history, your moods, your habits. Now imagine if therapy worked the same way: personalized, predictive, and adaptive in real time.

That is what artificial intelligence (AI) is bringing to digital therapeutics: the ability to tailor therapy not just to a disease, but to the individual living with it.

For decades, medicine has relied on averages. Drugs are tested on populations, doses are standardized, and guidelines are written for the "typical" patient. But in reality, no patient is typical. Each brings unique genetics, behaviors, and environments to their condition.

Digital therapeutics, powered by AI, are breaking that mold.

From Standard to Adaptive Therapy

Traditional CBT for insomnia, for instance, follows a set program: adjusting sleep schedules, changing habits, and monitoring progress. But what if the patient responds well to some interventions and not others? AI can detect patterns—when the patient struggles most, when engagement drops, and when improvement plateaus—and adjust the therapy in real-time.

- Somryst®, for example, is beginning to integrate adaptive algorithms that refine sleep modules based on patient progress, ensuring that therapy evolves in tandem with the patient's progress.

This is personalization at scale—something human therapists struggle to provide consistently.

Predicting Risk before it Happens

AI doesn't just personalize therapy; it predicts problems.

- Propeller Health uses machine learning to analyze inhaler use, weather, and pollution data. It can predict an asthma flare-up days before it happens and alert the patient to adjust medication or avoid triggers. For a child with severe asthma, that prediction isn't just data—it's prevention of an ER visit.

Tailoring Mental Health Interventions

Mental health, notoriously variable across individuals, has seen some of the most striking applications.

- Woebot Health, an AI-driven chatbot, adapts conversations to a patient's tone, mood, and behavior. Unlike static therapy modules, Woebot learns—offering reassurance, reframing thoughts, and delivering CBT techniques in ways that feel natural and personal.

The magic isn't that it talks. It's that it learns how to talk to you.

The Lesson

AI transforms digital therapeutics from being programs that are delivered to being programs that evolve. The more a patient uses them, the smarter they get—nudging, predicting, and personalizing therapy in ways static medicine never could.

Where pharma once sold the same pill to millions, AI-enabled DTx offers millions of different therapy experiences—each tailored to the individual.

The promise of AI in digital therapeutics extends beyond efficiency. It's intimacy. Therapy that knows when you're struggling, predicts when you might relapse, adapts when you plateau, and encourages when you waver.

In a healthcare system built on averages, AI is writing a new script: one where every patient receives a treatment plan that feels tailored just for them.

The Shift: From Static to Dynamic Therapy

Traditional medicine is static. A pill has one dosage. A device has one function. Even therapy sessions follow pre-set structures. Digital therapeutics, when powered by AI, wearables, and emerging tech, are dynamic—they learn, adapt, and evolve alongside the patient.

Imagine:

- A program for depression that adjusts its tone depending on your mood that day.
- A back pain app that corrects your posture in real time, using your phone's camera.
- An asthma sensor that warns you of a flare-up hours before it happens.

This is no longer speculation. These systems already exist in the real world.

The Role of Emerging Technologies

Each technology adds a layer of power:

- AI personalizes therapy, learning what works for each patient.
- Machine learning finds hidden patterns, predicting risk before symptoms worsen.
- Wearables collect continuous data, making therapy part of everyday life.
- Blockchain ensures trust by securing sensitive health data.
- Telemedicine integrates it all, connecting patients and providers seamlessly.

Together, they transform digital therapeutics from "apps that help" into ecosystems of care that anticipate, adapt, and protect.

Closing Thought

The story of AI and emerging technologies in digital therapeutics is the story of medicine moving closer to the patient—more responsive, more predictive, more personal.

Where traditional medicine treats you when you're sick, AI-enabled digital therapeutics aim to keep you well. And in that shift lies their most disruptive power: turning therapy from something you receive into something that lives with you, learns from you, and evolves for you.

6.1 The Role of AI in Personalizing Digital Therapeutics

One evening in San Francisco, a woman with chronic insomnia opened an app her doctor had prescribed: Somryst®. At first, it appeared to be a digital workbook—complete with sleep diaries, behavioral prompts, and exercises designed to reshape habits. But soon she noticed something curious: the app was learning her. On nights she reported high anxiety, she adjusted, slowing down the pace of cognitive exercises. When her sleep improved, the program advanced to more challenging modules.

This wasn't a static program. It was therapy that adapted—guided not by a human therapist, but by artificial intelligence.

Medicine Built on Averages

Traditional medicine treats patients as members of a group. A pill comes in a fixed dose. Therapy is delivered in a standardized sequence. Guidelines are designed for "most people." But no one is really average. Each patient brings unique habits, rhythms, and contexts.

AI allows digital therapeutics to break free from this one-size-fits-all model. By learning from an individual's data—such as sleep logs, movement patterns, mood reports, and even language—it can tailor therapy to the patient, rather than the population.

Therapy that Learns You

- EndeavorRx®, the ADHD video game, doesn't just entertain. It uses AI to monitor a child's response times, mistakes, and attention lapses. The difficulty adjusts in real time. For one child, the game slows down; for another, it ramps up. The therapy becomes a mirror of the child's unique cognitive profile.
- Woebot Health, an AI-driven chatbot for mental health, listens closely to how users type. The sentiment, tone, and even pauses in conversation shape its responses. If frustration creeps in, Woebot becomes more gentle. If progress shines through, it celebrates. Patients describe it as "talking to something that actually understands"—even though it's code, not a counselor.

From Reactive to Predictive

AI also shifts therapy from reacting to symptoms to anticipating them.

- Propeller Health merges inhaler use data with weather and air quality patterns. Its algorithms can alert asthma patients to risks before they experience wheezing or coughing. In effect, the therapeutic experience begins before the flare-up does.
- Kaia Health utilizes AI-driven motion tracking through a smartphone camera for managing chronic back pain. It doesn't just show exercises—it corrects form, prevents injury, and adapts to the patient's growing strength.

Here, personalization isn't a nice-to-have feature—it's the therapy itself.

Scaling Human Empathy

The irony of AI in medicine is that it makes digital therapeutics feel more human. A therapist might see you once a week. An app powered by AI can notice your struggles every day, at midnight or during a morning commute, and respond instantly.

Personalization at this scale was once thought to be impossible. With AI, it becomes the baseline.

The Lesson

AI personalizes digital therapeutics by moving them from programs you follow to companions that follow you. They adapt when you stumble, accelerate when you improve, and anticipate when you might relapse.

It transforms therapy from something you fit into to something that fits you.

Closing Thought

The great promise of AI in digital therapeutics isn't just smarter software. It's care that feels uniquely yours. Therapy that acknowledges your struggles, celebrates your progress, and adapts as needed.

In a healthcare system built for the average patient, AI whispers a radical idea: there is no average patient—there is only you.

6.2 Machine Learning Algorithms and Predictive Analytics in Therapeutic Design

In Chicago, a middle-aged man with COPD once dreaded winters. Cold air and flu season often sent him to the emergency room, gasping for breath. Then his doctor enrolled him in a program with Propeller Health. A tiny sensor on his inhaler, connected to machine learning algorithms, began tracking his usage and overlaying it with local weather, pollen, and pollution data.

One morning, his phone buzzed—not because he was already struggling, but because the system had predicted he soon would. It advised him to take precautions, adjust his schedule, and keep his inhaler close. That winter, for the first time in years, he avoided the ER.

This is the power of machine learning in digital therapeutics: the ability not only to guide therapy but also to forecast risk, adapt design, and prevent crises before they occur.

From Retrospective to Predictive Care

Traditional medicine often looks backward. Doctors review charts, test results, and symptoms that have already occurred. Digital therapeutics, infused with machine learning, look to the future. They see patterns invisible to the human eye, drawn from streams of data.

- Omada Health analyzes weight, glucose, and activity data from thousands of participants. Its algorithms identify which patients are most at risk of diabetes progression and adjust coaching intensity accordingly. Instead of treating everyone the same, Omada focuses resources where they matter most.
- In mental health, predictive analytics are being built into CBT-based platforms like Happify Health, identifying early signs of disengagement and offering nudges before patients abandon therapy altogether.

The shift is profound: From medicine that waits for decline, to medicine that anticipates it.

Designing Smarter Therapies

Machine learning doesn't just predict outcomes—it also shapes design.

- Kaia Health, in its digital back pain program, utilizes AI to track patient movements using a smartphone camera. But its predictive analytics go deeper: by analyzing adherence patterns, it can redesign exercises or adjust difficulty before patients lose motivation. The therapy evolves, not as a static program, but as a continuously improving system.
- reSET®, Pear Therapeutics' program for substance use disorder, uses predictive modeling to identify when patients are most at risk of relapse—nudging them with targeted modules or reminders at the exact moments they're needed most.

Here, machine learning becomes the invisible architect of the therapeutic journey.

The Lesson

Machine learning and predictive analytics give digital therapeutics three superpowers:

1. **Foresight:** Spotting risks before they become crises.
2. **Adaptability:** Refining interventions based on patterns of use and response.
3. **Efficiency:** Focusing resources on the patients most likely to benefit.

This transforms therapeutic design from being static and prescriptive to being dynamic and responsive.

Closing Thought

The story of predictive analytics in digital therapeutics is the story of medicine's shift from hindsight to foresight. Instead of asking, What went wrong, these algorithms ask, What might go wrong—and how do we stop it?

For the man in Chicago, it meant fewer ER visits. For patients with diabetes, it means slowing progression. For those in recovery, it means catching relapse before it begins.

And for medicine as a whole, it signals a new era: where the smartest therapy is not the one that reacts, but the one that already knows what's coming.

6.3 Wearable Technology and Remote Monitoring: Enhancing Patient Engagement

In 2014, a teenage boy in California collapsed during basketball practice. His Apple Watch, which he'd been wearing more as a style statement than a medical device, detected an abnormal heart rhythm and alerted him. Doctors later confirmed it had caught the onset of a rare condition early enough to intervene. What began as a consumer gadget had, in that moment, become a life-saving medical companion.

That story captures the essence of wearable technology in digital therapeutics: devices that don't just collect data but engage patients in their own care—transforming therapy from something episodic into something continuous.

From Occasional to Continuous Care

Traditional healthcare touches patients sporadically—an appointment here, a prescription refill there. Wearables collapse those gaps. They track heart rates, sleep cycles, glucose levels, and movement patterns every hour of every day.

- Dexcom's continuous glucose monitor (CGM) transmits blood sugar readings in real-time, alerting patients to potential dangerous spikes or drops. For people with diabetes, it's not just data—it's freedom from constant finger pricks.
- Fitbit and the Apple Watch initially started as lifestyle devices, but clinical studies have demonstrated their potential in tracking arrhythmias, sleep apnea, and even the early signs of COVID-19.

Engagement isn't forced. It's woven into daily life.

Extending the Reach of Digital Therapeutics

Wearables serve as sensors that make digital therapeutics more intelligent.

- Propeller Health pairs inhaler sensors with apps, turning every puff into a data point. Patients see their usage patterns; doctors see adherence trends. Engagement rises because feedback is instant and tangible.
- Kaia Health, which treats back pain, now integrates with motion sensors in smartphones and wearable devices. Patients receive real-time

corrections to their posture and exercise form—essentially a physical therapist in their pocket.

By giving patients immediate feedback, wearables turn passive users into active participants.

Remote Monitoring as a Safety Net

For clinicians, wearables offer something revolutionary: visibility into life between visits.

- In heart failure management, wearables like BioIntelliSense's BioSticker continuously track vital signs, sending alerts if patients show signs of decompensation. Instead of waiting for hospitalization, doctors can intervene early.
- During the COVID-19 pandemic, remote monitoring platforms allowed clinicians to track oxygen saturation in quarantined patients, providing reassurance and early detection of deterioration.

What was once invisible—the daily ups and downs of a patient's condition—is now transparent, trackable, and actionable.

The Engagement Effect

The most important contribution of wearables is psychological. Patients who have access to their data become partners in their own care. A diabetic watching a glucose graph dip after exercise feels empowered. A patient with COPD who notices fewer inhaler alerts over time sees progress made visible.

Engagement is no longer about willpower—it's about feedback. And feedback, delivered instantly, is one of the most powerful motivators in behavior change.

The Lesson

Wearables and remote monitoring transform digital therapeutics by:

1. Capturing continuous data, filling the gaps between clinical visits.
2. Delivering real-time feedback, making patients active participants.
3. Providing safety nets, alerting doctors before crises occur.

The result is deeper engagement, stronger adherence, and better outcomes.

Closing Thought

When healthcare is limited to hospitals, it overlooks the quiet moments where health is made or lost. Wearables bring medicine into those moments—onto wrists, into pockets, woven into daily routines.

For patients, this means therapy that doesn't wait for appointments. For clinicians, it means visibility into the invisible. For digital therapeutics, it means the difference between being used occasionally and being lived every day.

Engagement, once healthcare's biggest challenge, may finally have met its match—not in more reminders, but in devices that turn life itself into therapy.

6.4 Blockchain for Secure Data Management in Digital Therapeutics

In 2017, a major U.S. health insurer revealed that hackers had stolen the records of nearly 80 million patients. It wasn't just names and addresses—it was diagnoses, prescriptions, and medical histories. For those patients, the breach wasn't an abstract loss of privacy. It was the fear that their most personal vulnerabilities had become public property.

That story underscores why trust is as vital to digital therapeutics as efficacy. Patients will only engage with software that collects intimate health data if they believe it is secure, transparent, and under their control. And this is where blockchain enters the scene.

Why Blockchain?

At its core, blockchain is a digital ledger—an incorruptible chain of records distributed across multiple systems, rather than stored in a single vulnerable database. Once data is entered, it cannot be altered without leaving a trace. In healthcare, this means medical records that are immutable, transparent, and verifiable.

For digital therapeutics, where data is both the raw material (collected from patients) and the output (evidence of outcomes), blockchain promises two critical assurances:

1. Security – Data cannot be secretly tampered with.
2. Ownership – Patients, not corporations, can control access to their own records.

Practical Examples

- BurstIQ, a Colorado-based company, utilizes blockchain technology to securely manage patient health data, creating what it calls "smart contracts" that enable patients to determine who can access specific parts of their data.
- In Europe, blockchain-backed pilots for clinical trial transparency have ensured that data from DTx studies cannot be manipulated post-hoc—a critical factor for trust in regulatory submissions.

- For digital therapeutics like Propeller Health or Kaia Health, blockchain could serve as the backbone, ensuring that inhaler adherence data or back pain exercise logs are not only accurate but verifiable by insurers and regulators.

Trust as Engagement

In digital therapeutics, engagement depends not just on design or AI, but on trust. A patient with depression using Deprexis might share daily mood logs. A diabetic using a connected digital therapeutic (DTx) might upload their glucose readings. If they fear that data will be sold to advertisers or altered by error, engagement collapses.

Blockchain turns this equation on its head: it reassures patients that their data trail is permanent, transparent, and under their control. That reassurance isn't cosmetic—it's therapeutic, because without it, patients will disengage.

The Lesson

Blockchain does not directly make a digital therapeutic more effective in treating a disease. But it makes it trustworthy—and in digital medicine, trust is as essential as efficacy.

- AI personalizes therapy.
- Wearables extend therapy.
- Blockchain protects therapy.

Together, they create not just smarter care, but safer care.

Closing Thought

For centuries, medicine has relied on trust between patient and doctor. Digital therapeutics extend that relationship into the digital realm, where an app often represents the doctor and the therapy resides in code. Blockchain ensures that trust is not eroded but reinforced—by making data secure, ownership transparent, and evidence incorruptible.

Because, in the end, patients won't care how clever the algorithm is if they don't trust the system that holds their data. Blockchain ensures they can.

6.5 Telemedicine Integration: Expanding the Reach of Digital Therapeutics

In April 2020, at the height of the COVID-19 pandemic, a patient in rural Kentucky had her first therapy session for anxiety—not in an office, but on her phone. Her psychiatrist, hundreds of miles away, prescribed not just medication but also access to Deprexis, a digital therapeutic for depression and anxiety. Within minutes, she had two forms of care—pharmaceutical and digital—delivered through a single telemedicine platform.

That moment illustrates the quiet revolution of telemedicine integration: digital therapeutics becoming part of the virtual doctor's toolkit, accessible wherever the patient is.

From Point Solutions to Connected Care

Before the advent of telemedicine, digital therapeutics often operated in silos. Patients downloaded an app from an app store or received a code from a trial. Physicians struggled to monitor progress, and payers hesitated to reimburse because integration was clumsy.

Telemedicine changed that dynamic. When DTx are prescribed and monitored through telehealth platforms, they cease to be isolated tools and become part of the care continuum.

- Teladoc Health has experimented with integrating behavioral digital therapeutics into its virtual psychiatry visits, offering patients immediate access to CBT-based programs alongside therapy sessions.
- In Europe, Germany's DiGA Fast-Track enables doctors to prescribe approved digital therapeutic (DTx) products during telemedicine visits, with insurers reimbursing costs in the same manner as they would for traditional medications.

The result is seamlessness: patients leave a virtual appointment with therapy in hand, not just advice to "look something up."

Expanding Reach Across Geography

Telemedicine is, above all, an equalizer. It dissolves geography. For patients in rural areas or in countries with specialist shortages, it opens doors that physical clinics cannot.

- A COPD patient in Montana can connect with a pulmonologist in Denver, receive an inhaler prescription, and simultaneously enroll in Propeller Health's DTx—all in one telemedicine session.
- A child with ADHD in a small town can see a specialist virtually, get a prescription for EndeavorRx®, and begin therapy the same week, instead of waiting months for an appointment.

In both cases, integration ensures DTx are not "extras" patients must discover on their own—they are prescribed as standard care.

The Data Loop: Closing the Gap

Telemedicine also strengthens feedback loops. When digital therapeutics feed data back into telehealth platforms, physicians can monitor progress in real time.

- A doctor prescribing Somryst® for insomnia doesn't have to wait weeks for a patient's self-report. Usage and outcomes are displayed in dashboards, enabling more precise follow-ups.
- In diabetes care, integrating DTx like Omada Health into telemedicine means doctors can see glucose data, weight trends, and behavioral progress before the video visit begins.

The appointment stops being a recap of the past and becomes a conversation about the present—and the future.

The Lesson

Telemedicine integration transforms digital therapeutics in three ways:

1. Access – making them available to patients regardless of their geographical location.
2. Seamlessness – embedding them into the physician workflow.
3. Continuity – feeding data back into care, closing the loop between patient and provider.

What was once fragmented becomes fluid.

Closing Thought

For centuries, healthcare was bound by geography. Patients traveled to doctors. Therapies were dispensed in person. Telemedicine—and its marriage with digital therapeutics—breaks that chain.

Now, therapy travels to the patient. Care is prescribed, delivered, and monitored through screens. And in that shift, digital therapeutics expand from niche tools into mainstream medicine—not because they replaced traditional care, but because telemedicine made them part of it.

The future of therapy may not be found in the clinic at all. It may be found in the quiet space between a patient's living room and a doctor's office, miles away, and the app that connects them both.

Chapter 7

Measuring the Success of Digital Therapeutics

In Silicon Valley, success is often measured in downloads, daily active users, or time spent on an app. However, in healthcare, those metrics overlook the key point. A meditation app can boast millions of downloads, yet never prove it reduces depression. A step counter can gamify walking, yet it fails to demonstrate that it lowers cardiovascular risk.

Digital therapeutics operate in a distinct realm. They aren't judged by popularity. They're judged the way drugs are: Do they work? Do they improve lives? Do they save costs?

That's why measuring success in digital therapeutics is not about vanity metrics. It is about outcomes—clinical, behavioral, and economic.

Key Performance Indicators (KPIs) for Digital Therapeutics

The first step is defining what to measure. Unlike wellness apps, where engagement might be enough, DTx requires KPIs that mirror medicine:

- **Clinical endpoints:** Did insomnia patients fall asleep faster with Somryst®?
- Did ADHD children improve attention with EndeavorRx®?
- **Behavioral change:** Did patients with diabetes in Omada's program sustain healthier eating and exercise habits?
- **Adherence:** Did COPD patients actually use their inhalers consistently with Propeller Health?

- **Economic value:** Did the DTx reduce ER visits, hospitalizations, or long-term costs?

Success is not "more users." It's "better outcomes."

Patient Engagement and Adherence Metrics

Still, engagement matters—because without it, outcomes don't happen. A pill works when swallowed; a DTx works when used.

- Propeller Health tracked not just inhaler adherence but also app interactions. Patients who used the system regularly saw 50% fewer hospitalizations.
- Kaia Health measured completion of back pain exercises, showing that patients who engaged with the app at least three times per week reported significantly lower pain scores.

Engagement in DTx isn't about screen time—it's about therapeutic time: moments when the patient is actively practicing behaviors that reinforce outcomes.

Clinical and Economic Outcomes: Demonstrating Value to Stakeholders

No payer will reimburse, no physician will prescribe, unless the therapy proves its value.

- Omada Health demonstrated that its diabetes prevention program reduced progression to Type 2 diabetes and cut long-term healthcare costs—data that convinced insurers to cover it.
- Deprexis showed reductions in depressive symptoms comparable to face-to-face CBT, positioning it as a viable alternative where therapists are scarce.

Clinical outcomes win regulatory approval. Economic outcomes win reimbursement. Together, they win legitimacy.

Real-World Evidence (RWE) and Post-Market Surveillance

The final test of success is what happens outside the lab. Randomized controlled trials help determine whether a digital therapeutic (DTx) is approved, but real-world evidence ultimately determines whether it is successful.

- In Germany, products listed under the DiGA Fast-Track must submit ongoing real-world data to demonstrate continued effectiveness and remain reimbursed. This ensures DTx doesn't just work in trials but in everyday life.
- Pear's reSET® gathered post-market data on abstinence rates, refining its program and proving sustained impact beyond the initial studies.

RWE is the bridge between regulatory approval and lasting adoption. It reassures payers, clinicians, and patients that success isn't theoretical—it's lived.

The Lesson

Measuring success in digital therapeutics requires a new playbook:

- Clinical impact – Are symptoms reduced? Are conditions managed better?
- Behavioral impact – Are patients adhering to therapy, changing their habits, and sustaining these changes?
- Economic impact – Are costs lower, ER visits fewer, outcomes stronger?
- Real-world proof – Do results hold outside the trial?

Without these, even the most elegant software is just another app. With them, it becomes medicine.

Closing Thought

For a century, drugs have been judged by the rigor of trials and the strength of outcomes. Digital therapeutics demand the same—but add new dimensions: engagement, behavior, and continuous data.

In this way, measuring success is not a hurdle. It is the essence of legitimacy. Because the real triumph of digital therapeutics won't be measured in app stores or downloads, but in nights of sleep restored, relapses prevented, hospital visits avoided, and lives lived better.

That's the metric that matters.

7.1 Key Performance Indicators (KPIs) for Digital Therapeutics

In the early days of fitness apps, success was measured by the number of downloads. If a million people installed your step counter, you were celebrated. However, when researchers examined the data more closely, they discovered a sobering truth: most people abandoned the app within weeks. Engagement was fleeting, outcomes nonexistent.

Digital therapeutics can't afford that kind of vanity metric. They're not judged by how many people install them, but by whether they change health trajectories. The KPIs for DTx aren't likes or log-ins. They are clinical, behavioral, and economic outcomes that mirror the rigor of medicine itself.

Clinical Outcomes: Does it Work Like a Drug?

The gold standard for any therapeutic, digital or chemical, is simple: does it improve the condition?

- Somryst® tracked sleep latency and wake time. Success was measured in minutes gained: patients falling asleep faster and staying asleep longer.
- EndeavorRx®, the ADHD video game, measured improvement in attention scores compared to baseline. Clinical endpoints—not engagement—drove its FDA approval.

Here, the KPI isn't usage time. It's symptom reduction, measured with the same discipline applied to drugs.

Behavioral Outcomes: Are Patients Adhering to Treatment?

But digital therapeutics add another dimension: adherence to the therapy itself. A pill works when swallowed; a DTx works when used.

- Propeller Health didn't just measure inhaler puffs. It measured consistent inhaler use over time. The KPI was adherence, which correlated directly with a decrease in ER visits.
- Kaia Health tracked exercise completion rates among patients with back pain. Those who performed app-guided exercises at least three times per week reported significantly lower pain scores.

In this sense, KPIs in DTx encompass the behaviors that drive the outcome.

Engagement Metrics: Not Vanity, but Therapeutic

Engagement still matters—but not in the way Silicon Valley defines it. More clicks or longer screen time aren't the goal. The goal is meaningful therapeutic engagement.

- reSET®, Pear Therapeutics 'substance use disorder DTx, measured "completion of therapeutic modules" as a KPI. Patients who finished more modules showed higher abstinence rates.
- In Omada Health's diabetes program, sustained weight loss wasn't just the outcome—it was tied to the KPI of how often patients logged meals and weighed themselves.

Here, engagement is not a distraction. It's medicine in action.

Economic Outcomes: is it Worth Paying for?

Payers want to know: Does the therapy save money?

- Omada Health published data showing its diabetes prevention program cut progression rates and reduced long-term healthcare costs. That economic KPI was key to securing insurer contracts.
- In Germany's DiGA Fast-Track, reimbursement for DTx depends on demonstrating "positive healthcare effects"—a KPI that blends clinical improvement with cost-effectiveness.

For DTx, proving economic value is not optional—it's survival.

The Lesson

The KPIs for digital therapeutics aren't borrowed from tech. They're borrowed from medicine—augmented with behavior and economics.

1. Clinical outcomes – measurable improvements in symptoms.
2. Behavioral outcomes – adherence and therapeutic use.
3. Engagement – but defined as meaningful participation, not time spent.
4. Economic outcomes – reduced costs, improved value for payers.

Together, these create a picture of whether a digital therapeutic is not just being used, but actually working in the real world.

Closing Thought

If a million people download a meditation app and no one gets better, is it a success? In healthcare, the answer is no.

Digital therapeutics flip the script: their success isn't about scale alone, but about outcomes achieved at scale. Their KPIs are the proof that software can sit alongside drugs, not as a novelty, but as real medicine.

7.2 Patient Engagement and Adherence Metrics

In 2019, a study of digital health apps revealed a sobering finding: more than half of users abandoned them within two weeks. The novelty wore off, reminders felt intrusive, and the apps became another icon buried on the phone's screen.

For a step counter, that might not be a concern. But for a digital therapeutic, abandonment is fatal. Unlike a pill, which delivers chemistry with every swallow, a DTx only works when patients actually use it. Engagement isn't decoration—it's the therapy itself.

The Difference between Logging in and Leaning in

Engagement in DTx isn't measured by how often someone opens the app, but by whether they interact meaningfully with the therapy.

- reSET® (Pear Therapeutics 'substance use disorder DTx) tracked module completion as a KPI. Patients who finished more lessons had significantly higher abstinence rates than those who dropped out early. Engagement directly predicted recovery.
- Somryst, for insomnia, measured adherence to CBT-I exercises, including keeping sleep diaries and completing behavioral tasks. App visits didn't define success, but by patients faithfully following the therapy's rhythm night after night.

The lesson: in digital therapeutics, engagement is never vanity. It's dosage.

Adherence as the Invisible Battle

In chronic disease, adherence has always been the billion-dollar blind spot. Patients forget pills, skip appointments, and abandon diets. Digital therapeutics make adherence measurable.

- Propeller Health transformed inhaler adherence from an invisible behavior into a visible metric. Its sensors tracked every puff, and adherence reports showed which patients were struggling to adhere to their treatment regimen. With reminders and coaching, adherence rose—and ER visits fell.

- Kaia Health, in back pain management, measured how often patients completed exercise sessions. Those who adhered to at least three sessions a week reported far better outcomes. The metric wasn't app installs—it was sustained participation.

Adherence is no longer a mystery. It's a metric that predicts outcomes.

Designing for Stickiness

Engagement and adherence don't happen by accident. They are designed into the therapy.

- EndeavorRx®, the ADHD video game, disguised therapy as play. Children returned not out of obligation, but because they wanted to. Engagement was engineered into the mechanics.
- Omada Health built accountability into its diabetes program, where patients weighed in weekly, received coaching, and compared their progress with that of their peers. That social loop maintained high adherence over time.

The insight here is from behavioral science: when therapy feels rewarding, personalized, and connected, adherence tends to follow.

The Lesson

For digital therapeutics, patient engagement and adherence metrics are not side notes. They are the lifeblood of efficacy.

- Engagement measures whether patients are interacting meaningfully with the therapy.
- Adherence measures whether they sustain that interaction long enough for outcomes to emerge.

Together, they determine whether the software is actually functioning as medicine.

Closing Thought

In traditional medicine, adherence is a hope—"take your pills as directed." In digital therapeutics, adherence is a metric—visible, trackable, improvable.

That visibility changes everything. It means companies can design for engagement, physicians can monitor progress, and patients can see their own commitment reflected in data.

And in that loop of measurement, feedback, and reinforcement lies the power of digital therapeutics: not just prescribing behavior change, but sustaining it.

7.3 Clinical and Economic Outcomes: Demonstrating Value to Stakeholders

In 2018, an insurer reviewing claims data noticed something unusual. Members enrolled in Omada Health's digital diabetes prevention program weren't just losing weight—they were filing fewer hospital claims, needing fewer medications, and costing the system less. What began as a digital coaching app for lifestyle changes had quietly become a financial lever for the insurer.

That story highlights the central truth for digital therapeutics: clinical success is necessary, but economic value makes them sustainable. In healthcare, therapies survive not only because they are effective, but also because they yield a return on investment.

Clinical Outcomes: The First Proof

Stakeholders—patients, physicians, regulators—start with one question: Does it make people healthier?

- Somryst, used to treat chronic insomnia, demonstrated reductions in sleep latency and nighttime wakefulness that persisted for months after use—proving the durability of its outcomes beyond those of traditional sleep medications.
- EndeavorRx, for pediatric ADHD, improved attention scores in clinical trials, demonstrating measurable benefits comparable to those of pharmacological interventions.
- Deprexis, in Europe, reduced depressive symptoms to levels on par with in-person cognitive behavioral therapy, making it a lifeline where therapists are scarce.

These clinical outcomes win regulatory approval and physician confidence. They prove that digital therapeutics are more than polished apps—they are medicine.

Economic Outcomes: The Decisive Factor

But for payers and health systems, clinical proof alone isn't enough. They need to know: Does it save money?

- Propeller Health demonstrated that patients with asthma and COPD who used its inhaler sensors experienced fewer hospitalizations and ER visits. Fewer emergencies meant lower costs, creating a compelling case for insurer reimbursement.
- Omada Health quantified reductions in progression to Type 2 diabetes, translating clinical wins into hard-dollar savings for insurers—savings large enough to justify coverage.
- In Germany, the DiGA Fast-Track explicitly ties reimbursement to "positive healthcare effects," requiring DTx to demonstrate not just health improvements but cost offsets compared to standard care.

For payers, this is the KPI that matters most: better outcomes at lower or at least sustainable cost.

The Stakeholder Equation

Each stakeholder defines value differently:

- Patients want improved symptoms and quality of life.
- Physicians want tools that complement their care and show real-world results.
- Payers want lower costs and fewer claims.
- Pharma wants differentiation and stronger brand value.

Digital therapeutics must meet all these needs simultaneously. That's why success is measured on dual axes: clinical impact and economic sustainability.

The Lesson

Digital therapeutics that deliver only clinical outcomes risk being seen as boutique tools—effective but unaffordable. Those that deliver only economic outcomes risk being dismissed as cost-cutting gimmicks. The winners deliver both: measurable symptom relief and demonstrable cost savings.

This is the formula that convinces stakeholders.

Closing Thought

In traditional medicine, the gap between clinical efficacy and economic value was often wide. A drug could work wonders yet bankrupt patients or health systems. Digital therapeutics offer a rare convergence: the chance to improve lives while lowering costs.

For stakeholders, that combination is irresistible. And for digital therapeutics, it is the path from experimental novelty to mainstream medicine.

7.4 Real-World Evidence (RWE) and Post-Market Surveillance

In the late 1990s, the world celebrated a blockbuster painkiller that promised relief without the side effects of older drugs. Clinical trials had looked strong. Regulators approved it. Sales soared. But in the real world, patterns emerged: patients on the drug had higher rates of heart attacks and strokes. By the time the product was pulled, millions had been exposed.

That history left medicine with a lesson: clinical trials show what happens in controlled environments. But real life is messy. To truly know how a therapy works, you need real-world evidence.

For digital therapeutics, that lesson is amplified. Their success isn't just in the trial. It's whether patients actually use them daily, whether the outcomes last, and whether the data continues to prove value long after launch.

Why Real-World Evidence Matters

Randomized controlled trials (RCTs) are used to evaluate the effectiveness of a therapy and determine its approval. But RCTs are artificial—they select patients, control conditions, and exclude complexity. Real-world evidence, by contrast, captures what happens in everyday life:

- Do asthma patients actually use their inhalers with Propeller Health outside trial settings?
- Does Omada Health's diabetes program still reduce progression rates after two years in the wild, not just six months in a study?
- Do insomnia patients using Somryst® keep their improved sleep patterns months later, when the novelty has worn off?

RWE answers these questions—and stakeholders demand it.

Germany's DiGA Model: Continuous Proof

Germany's DiGA Fast-Track takes RWE seriously. To remain reimbursed, digital therapeutics must continue to provide data showing "positive healthcare effects." In other words, approval isn't permanent—it's conditional on real-world performance.

This system has compelled companies like Kaia Health and HelloBetter not only to win trials but also to establish continuous evidence pipelines, demonstrating the effectiveness of their digital therapeutics (DTx) solutions across diverse populations.

Post-Market Surveillance: Catching the Gaps

Post-market surveillance adds another layer, involving the monitoring of safety and reliability once the product is in use.

- If a bug in Somryst® were to disrupt therapy sequences, post-market monitoring would detect it.
- If usage data showed that certain groups—such as older patients—were disengaging more quickly, companies could adapt their design, and regulators could update their guidance.

Unlike drugs, which remain chemically stable, DTx evolve through updates. Post-market surveillance ensures that evolution improves safety and efficacy rather than undermining them.

The Lesson

For digital therapeutics, RWE and surveillance are not afterthoughts. They are part of the therapeutic design itself. They:

1. Validate efficacy beyond trials, in messy, diverse, everyday life.
2. Demonstrate durability of outcomes—that results last, not fade.
3. Ensure safety in an evolving product, where updates can change algorithms overnight.

Without RWE, DTx risk is being dismissed as "trial toys." With it, they become trusted parts of mainstream medicine.

Closing Thought

Clinical trials may open the door, but real-world evidence keeps it open. For digital therapeutics, success isn't defined by what happens in a lab or on a trial site—it's defined by what happens in living rooms, workplaces, and daily routines.

The true measure of a therapy is not how well it performs in perfect conditions, but how reliably it improves lives in imperfect ones.

That is why RWE and post-market surveillance aren't just boxes to check. They are the lifeline that sustains digital therapeutics, proving day after day, patient by patient, that code can truly be a cure.

Chapter 8

Overcoming Barriers to Adoption

When Pear Therapeutics launched reSET®, the first FDA-approved prescription digital therapeutic for substance use disorder, the headlines were glowing. Regulators had validated it, clinicians had trial data in hand, and patients had access to a new form of therapy. Yet, uptake was slow. Many doctors hesitated to prescribe it. Insurers dragged their feet on reimbursement. Patients were unsure how to trust an app that came with a prescription.

The lesson was clear: approval alone does not guarantee adoption. For digital therapeutics to succeed, they must overcome barriers not of science, but of culture, economics, and trust.

Addressing Healthcare Provider Concerns and Misconceptions

Doctors are trained to prescribe pills, not apps. To many, digital therapeutics initially appeared to be wellness tools disguised as medical language.

- Some physicians feared they would be responsible for tech troubleshooting instead of patient care.
- Others doubted whether patients would stick with an app as reliably as they might with medication.

Companies like Propeller Health solved this by making their technology nearly invisible. The inhaler sensor required no extra effort, and data flowed into dashboards that physicians already used. For doctors, the key was seamless integration, not more work.

Engaging Patients: Building Trust and Confidence

Patients, too, carried skepticism. Medicine had always come in bottles and devices—could therapy delivered by software really be trusted?

- EndeavorRx®, the ADHD video game, faced exactly this barrier. Parents wondered: Can a game truly be therapeutic? The breakthrough came when the FDA's approval and clinical trial data reassured families. For children, engagement wasn't the issue—they loved the gameplay. For parents, legitimacy was.
- In mental health, digital therapeutics like Deprexis gained traction by positioning themselves not as replacements for therapists but as companions, extending support to moments between appointments. Patients adopted it once they understood it wasn't "therapy or app"—it was therapy plus app.

Trust, more than design, determined adoption.

Reimbursement Challenges: Navigating Payer Policies

Perhaps the hardest barrier is financial. Without reimbursement, digital therapeutics become out-of-pocket expenses—limiting access and adoption.

- In the U.S., insurers were initially hesitant to cover reSET and Somryst, questioning their cost-effectiveness. Pear had to generate real-world evidence showing reduced hospitalizations and better long-term outcomes to win coverage.
- Germany's DiGA Fast-Track addressed this by creating a clear pathway: approved digital therapeutic (DTx) were listed in a national registry and reimbursed like drugs. Adoption soared because the financial barrier was removed.

The lesson: without payer buy-in, even the most effective DTx struggle to reach scale.

Legal and Ethical Considerations: Data Privacy, Consent, and Access

- In a world where data breaches make headlines, patients worry: who owns their health data? Can it be sold to advertisers? Could a glitch harm their therapy?
- HIPAA in the U.S. and GDPR in Europe established legal frameworks, but companies needed to go further—building transparency into their products.
- Some DTx, such as those in mental health, now include clear dashboards that show exactly what data is collected, who has access to it, and why.

For patients, ethical clarity is as critical as clinical efficacy. Without it, trust evaporates.

The Lesson

Adoption of digital therapeutics depends on four forces:

1. Physician trust – Are providers convinced this adds value, not burden?
2. Patient trust – Do patients believe this is real therapy, not just tech hype?
3. Payer trust – Do insurers see outcomes and cost savings that justify reimbursement?
4. Public trust – Are data, safety, and ethics safeguarded transparently?

Overcoming these barriers isn't a one-time hurdle—it's an ongoing negotiation of trust at every level.

Closing Thought

Every medical breakthrough in history—vaccines, antibiotics, organ transplants—faced skepticism before acceptance. Digital therapeutics are no different. They will earn their place not just by being effective, but by proving themselves trustworthy, reimbursable, and seamlessly integrated into the daily lives of patients and providers.

The real challenge isn't coding the therapy. It's convincing the world that code can truly be a form of medicine. And that battle is fought not in labs or trials, but in the hearts and minds of those who must prescribe, pay for, and use them.

8.1 Addressing Healthcare Provider Concerns and Misconceptions

When the first FDA-approved digital therapeutic, reSET®, appeared in 2017, many physicians reacted with a shrug. They weren't dismissing its science—they were uncertain about what it meant for their practice. How do I prescribe an app? Will I be responsible for tech support if something goes wrong? How do I fit digital therapy into my already overburdened workflow?

These weren't trivial questions. They reflected the underlying barrier to adoption: physicians trusted the clinical evidence, but they didn't yet trust the fit.

The Pill vs. The App

Doctors are trained to prescribe pills, injectables, and devices. They know the protocols, the dosage schedules, the side-effect profiles. Digital therapeutics introduced a new language—modules, log-ins, dashboards—that felt foreign.

- Psychiatrists worried that prescribing Deprexis for depression would lead to more patient confusion than patient benefit: What if the app stops working? What if the patient doesn't engage?
- Pulmonologists hesitated with Propeller Health, unsure if the inhaler sensor would complicate device handling or create more questions during visits.

The skepticism wasn't about efficacy. It was about disruption.

Making Technology Invisible

The digital therapeutics that succeeded early understood this: adoption happens when technology feels invisible.

- Propeller Health designed its inhaler sensor to be effortless—clip it on, use the inhaler as usual, let the data flow automatically into a dashboard. Doctors didn't have to explain how to use it; patients barely noticed it was there. Physicians received clean, actionable data that enhanced conversations, rather than distracting from them.
- Kaia Health, in back pain management, made its app self-guided and intuitive. By using the smartphone's camera as a motion coach, patients needed little hand-holding. Doctors could recommend it without fearing follow-up calls about setup or troubleshooting.

When technology respects clinical workflow, trust follows.

The Fear of Replacing the Clinician

Another misconception is that digital therapeutics will render doctors irrelevant. In reality, the best DTx are designed as adjuncts, not replacements.

- EndeavorRx® was never meant to replace pediatricians or psychiatrists. It was a complement—an evidence-based game prescribed alongside other treatments. Once physicians saw it positioned as therapy plus doctor rather than therapy instead of doctor, skepticism eased.
- Similarly, Deprexis presented itself as a bridge between therapy sessions, not a substitute for therapy itself. For clinicians facing waitlists, it became a tool to extend their reach.

Clarity of role—adjunct, not replacement—helped shift perceptions.

The Lesson

Healthcare provider skepticism isn't rooted in hostility to innovation. It's rooted in pragmatism. Doctors fear anything that adds friction to care or blurs accountability.

Overcoming their concerns requires:

1. Seamless integration – making DTx effortless to prescribe and monitor.
2. Clear role definition – positioning DTx as companions, not competitors.
3. Demonstrated value – showing how the data they generate improves clinical decision-making.

Closing Thought

Every major medical advance—from the stethoscope to electronic health records—was met with skepticism from providers before becoming indispensable. Digital therapeutics are on the same trajectory. Their adoption will hinge less on dazzling physicians with novelty and more on reassuring them with simplicity, clarity, and clinical relevance.

Ultimately, providers don't fear innovation. They fear distraction. And the DTx that succeeds will be the ones that feel less like gadgets and more like medicine.

8.2 Engaging Patients: Building Trust and Confidence in Digital Therapeutics

In 2020, when the FDA approved EndeavorRx, the first video game prescribed as a medicine, the reaction from many parents was one of disbelief. How could a game help my child's ADHD? One mother confessed: "I thought it was a gimmick. I worried I'd be wasting time when what my son needed was real therapy."

It took seeing her child's improvement—his attention scores rising, his engagement in school improving—for her skepticism to turn into trust. For patients and families, the leap from pill to program, from medicine to code, isn't automatic. It requires confidence not only in the science but in the experience.

The Trust Gap

Patients have always relied on the visible—the pill bottle, the injection, the therapy session. Digital therapeutics live in the invisible: algorithms, interfaces, data streams. That invisibility breeds doubt.

- Mental health apps face this barrier acutely. A patient with depression might ask: Can a chatbot really understand me?
- Diabetics offered digital coaching often wonder: Is this as good as seeing a doctor or a nutritionist face to face?

The hesitation isn't about technology—it's about legitimacy.

Legitimacy through Prescription

Trust rises when DTx are prescribed like medicine, not downloaded like apps.

- In Germany's DiGA Fast-Track, patients receive digital therapeutics through physician prescription and reimbursement by insurers. That framing—prescribed, covered, official—signals legitimacy. It tells patients: this isn't an experiment, it's healthcare.
- Deprexis, for depression, gained credibility when positioned not as "self-help software" but as a clinically validated adjunct to therapy. Patients felt safer engaging when they knew their doctors endorsed it.

Prescription turns novelty into necessity.

Confidence Through Design

The patient experience itself also matters. DTx must feel safe, clear, and empowering—not overwhelming.

- Propeller Health built patient confidence by giving instant feedback on inhaler use. Patients could see patterns, celebrate progress, and understand triggers. Engagement increased because therapy felt actionable, rather than abstract.
- Kaia Health gave back pain patients real-time corrections through motion tracking. Instead of asking them to "trust the program," it proved its worth by coaching them directly. Confidence came from seeing the app help in real time.

Trust isn't abstract—it's experiential. Patients believe when they see results in their daily lives.

The Lesson

Patient adoption of digital therapeutics requires three ingredients:

1. Legitimacy – delivered through prescription, approval, and reimbursement.
2. Clarity – positioning DTx as companions to care, not replacements.
3. Proof in use – experiences that show, quickly and tangibly, that the therapy works.

Without these, digital therapeutics risk being dismissed as gimmicks. With them, they become trusted partners in health.

Closing Thought

For patients, the journey to trust is not about algorithms or AI. It is about confidence: confidence that this is real therapy, that it respects their data, and that it improves their life.

Once that trust is earned, patients don't see digital therapeutics as "apps" anymore. They see them for what they truly are: medicine delivered in a new form.

8.3 Reimbursement Challenges: Navigating Payer Policies

When Pear Therapeutics secured FDA approval for reSET®, it was a historic milestone. The science was validated, regulators were convinced, and doctors could finally prescribe a digital therapeutic. Yet there was one problem: most insurers wouldn't pay for it. Patients were left to cover costs out of pocket, hundreds of dollars that many couldn't afford. Pear had created a medicine, but without reimbursement, it remained a medicine that few could access.

This tension—between clinical approval and financial adoption—is at the heart of digital therapeutics. For payers, the question isn't only does it work? But is it worth paying for?

The Payer's Perspective

Pharmaceutical companies know the drill: efficacy alone won't guarantee reimbursement. Payers want proof of value—that the therapy not only improves health but lowers long-term costs.

- Omada Health succeeded by publishing data showing its diabetes prevention program reduced the onset of Type 2 diabetes, saving insurers money on future complications. That economic story, not just the clinical one, convinced payers to cover it.
- By contrast, early mental health DTx often struggled. Payers questioned whether app-based CBT programs were simply "digital wellness" rather than reimbursable therapy. Without hard cost-offset data, coverage remained limited.

For insurers, outcomes without economics feel incomplete.

Different Markets, Different Models

Some regions have addressed this issue more effectively than others.

- Germany's DiGA Fast-Track has established a clear framework: if a digital therapeutic demonstrates "positive healthcare effects" through real-world evidence, it is listed in the national directory and reimbursed by insurers. Patients receive access as easily as they would for a prescription for a medication.

- The U.S., by contrast, remains patchy. Coverage varies by state and insurer. Some employers contract directly with DTx providers, such as Omada Health while others leave patients to cover the costs themselves. For developers, this fragmented landscape makes scaling painfully slow.

The difference between systems illustrates the barrier: without predictable reimbursement, DTx adoption remains inconsistent.

The Reimbursement Catch-22

Digital therapeutics face a paradox:

- Payers demand real-world evidence before reimbursement.
- But without reimbursement, adoption is too limited to generate robust real-world evidence.

This chicken-and-egg problem leaves many DTx in limbo—scientifically sound, regulator-approved, but commercially stranded. Companies often bridge the gap by partnering with pharma (for scale) or employers (for access) until insurers catch up.

The Lesson

Reimbursement is the make-or-break barrier for digital therapeutics. Overcoming it requires:

1. Clinical evidence – proving outcomes in trials.
2. Economic evidence – demonstrating cost savings in real-world use.
3. Policy innovation – frameworks like DiGA that create clarity and predictability.

Without these, adoption remains niche. With them, DTx can move from boutique solutions to mainstream medicine.

Closing Thought

In healthcare, approval earns attention. Reimbursement earns adoption. For digital therapeutics, this is the decisive hurdle: proving not just that they can heal, but that they can also pay their way.

Because in the end, no matter how clever the code or compelling the science, a therapy isn't truly medicine until insurers are willing to cover it—and patients can access it without cost becoming the barrier.

8.4 Legal and Ethical Considerations: Data Privacy, Consent, and Access

In 2019, a popular period-tracking app was exposed for quietly sharing user data with advertisers. What women believed to be private health information—intimate details about cycles, moods, and symptoms—was being traded as marketing currency. The backlash was swift. Millions deleted the app, and trust in digital health tools suffered a body blow.

For digital therapeutics, which rely on patients' daily trust to share sensitive health data, such a breach is existential. Without robust privacy protections, transparent consent, and equitable access, no amount of clinical evidence will matter. The question patients silently ask is not just "Does this work?" but "Can I trust this?"

The Privacy Imperative

Traditional drugs don't know who you are. Digital therapeutics do. They log behaviors, emotions, sleep cycles, glucose readings, even geolocation. That intimacy makes them powerful—and vulnerable.

- Propeller Health's inhaler sensors record every puff. Without airtight security, that data could expose a patient's medical condition to employers, insurers, or marketers.
- Mental health DTx like Woebot or Deprexis process conversations about anxiety, trauma, or depression. A breach here isn't just a loss of privacy—it's a violation of trust at the deepest level.

This is why frameworks like HIPAA in the U.S. and GDPR in Europe are non-negotiable. They ensure patient data is encrypted, anonymized, and accessible only to authorized parties.

The Consent Problem

Too often, patients click "I agree" without fully understanding what they are agreeing to. For digital therapeutics, informed consent must go beyond fine print.

- Some DTx now use clear, visual dashboards to show patients what data is collected, how it's used, and who sees it.

- Germany's DiGA Fast-Track requires digital therapeutic (DTx) providers to disclose their data practices explicitly before reimbursement approval.

The principle is simple: patients should never be surprised by how their data is handled.

The Question of Access

Ethics isn't just about privacy. It's about equity. If digital therapeutics are available only to those who can afford them out of pocket, they risk widening health disparities.

- In the U.S., patchy reimbursement means patients in wealthier areas are more likely to access DTx, while those in underserved communities are left behind.
- In Germany, by contrast, DiGA ensures equitable access through insurer coverage—any patient with a prescription gets the therapy, regardless of income.

Access is not just a business issue. It's an ethical one.

The Lesson

The legal and ethical backbone of digital therapeutics rests on three pillars:

1. Data privacy – protecting sensitive information from misuse or breach.
2. Informed consent – ensuring patients understand and control how their data is used.
3. Equitable access – guaranteeing that DTx are available to all, not just those who can afford them.

Neglect any of these, and adoption falters—not because of clinical failure, but because of eroded trust.

Closing Thought

Digital therapeutics promise a new intimacy in medicine—therapy that lives on your phone, learns from your habits, and travels with you day and night. But that intimacy cuts both ways. It can heal or betray.

Patients will only embrace digital therapeutics (DTx) when they believe their data is secure, their consent is respected, and their access is equitable. Because in digital medicine, trust isn't a feature. It's the treatment itself.

Chapter 9

The Future of Digital Therapeutics

In 2021, a small pilot study in Tokyo investigated whether a digital therapeutic could help cancer patients manage chemotherapy side effects. The program combined a smartphone app with AI-driven symptom tracking, wearable sensors, and virtual coaching. Within weeks, patients reported fewer ER visits, improved energy, and greater confidence in managing treatment. What struck researchers most wasn't just the outcomes—it was the sense that care had quietly shifted from the hospital to the home, from a reactive to a proactive approach.

That story captures the trajectory of digital therapeutics. What began as niche tools for insomnia, ADHD, or COPD is evolving into something far bigger: a new model of care. The future of digital therapeutics isn't about apps—it's about ecosystems.

Emerging Trends in Digital Therapeutics

The first wave of DTx proved the concept. The next wave is about expansion—across conditions, technologies, and geographies.

- **Multi-condition platforms:** Companies are moving beyond single-disease apps toward platforms addressing comorbidities. A diabetic patient may receive integrated support for sleep, anxiety, and weight management—because real patients rarely fit into one diagnostic box.
- **Combination therapies:** Pharma is increasingly bundling drugs with DTx as "digital-drug duets," where pills target biology and software targets behavior. Sanofi's partnerships in mental health and Roche's ventures in multiple sclerosis show the blueprint.
- **Gamified care:** EndeavorRx was just the start. Expect more therapies that feel like games, stories, or immersive experiences—where patients stay engaged because therapy doesn't feel like therapy at all.

The Role of Genomics and Personalized Medicine

The convergence of genomics and AI-powered digital therapeutics (DTx) promises precision therapy at scale. Imagine:

- A patient's genetic profile guides drug selection for cancer treatment.
- A digital therapeutic, tuned by AI, adapts daily behavioral interventions to that same patient's unique response pattern.

Here, personalization won't just mean tailoring therapy to symptoms—it will mean tailoring therapy to the patient's DNA and daily life simultaneously.

Global Expansion: Opportunities and Challenges in Emerging Markets

Digital therapeutics are spreading fastest where infrastructure gaps are greatest.

- In India, where doctor-to-patient ratios are stretched, DTx offers scalable solutions for diabetes and mental health.
- In Africa, mobile-first ecosystems enable the leapfrogging of traditional care models, allowing for the direct delivery of DTx to patients via smartphones.

The primary challenges are affordability and digital literacy. The opportunity is to create equitable access on a population scale, reaching patients who might otherwise be excluded from modern medicine.

The Evolving Relationship between Pharma, Tech Companies, and Healthcare Providers

The future of DTx will be written at the intersections.

- Pharma brings clinical expertise, regulatory muscle, and payer networks.
- Tech companies bring agility, design thinking, and data analytics.
- Providers bring patient trust and clinical integration.

When these groups collaborate, rather than compete, digital therapeutics stop being fringe experiments and become mainstream healthcare. The partnerships of Novartis–Pear, Sanofi–Happify, and Roche–Kaia Health are early signals of this shift.

Predictions for the Next Decade

Looking ahead, several trajectories are clear:

- Digital therapeutics will transition from adjuncts to frontline treatments in areas such as mental health, diabetes, and chronic pain.
- Regulatory pathways like DiGA will expand globally, normalizing reimbursement.
- AI, wearables, and genomics will converge, leading to hyper-personalized therapy.
- Patients will come to expect digital companions as part of every care plan, the way they once came to expect pills in bottles.

The endgame isn't replacing traditional medicine—it's rebalancing it: drugs for biology, digital for behavior, data for insight, all integrated into one system of care.

Closing Thought

The future of digital therapeutics won't be defined by algorithms or devices alone. It will be defined by whether they can win trust, demonstrate value, and scale equitably across societies.

If they succeed, medicine in the 2030s may look radically different. Therapy will not be confined to clinics or pharmacies. It will live on wrists, in pockets, and in the rhythms of daily life.

And when that happens, the story of digital therapeutics won't be about apps at all. It will be about a new kind of medicine—one that learns, adapts, and stays with us, not just when we are sick, but every day in between.

9.1 Emerging Trends in Digital Therapeutics

In 2022, a health start-up in Berlin launched a program for patients with diabetes. However, unlike earlier digital therapeutics, which focused on a single issue—such as blood sugar tracking or weight loss—this one was multi-layered. It monitored glucose, delivered mental health modules to address stress, offered sleep hygiene lessons, and encouraged daily activity. The idea was simple but profound: patients don't live in silos, so why should their therapies?

That story reflects one of the defining trends in digital therapeutics: expansion. What began as narrow, condition-specific tools is evolving into holistic ecosystems that meet patients across multiple dimensions of health.

From Single-Condition to Multi-Condition Platforms

The earliest DTx were laser-focused—insomnia (Somryst®), ADHD (EndeavorRx®), substance use (reSET®). Today, the movement is toward integrated platforms.

- Omada Health, once focused on diabetes prevention, now addresses obesity, hypertension, and mental health—all under one digital roof.
- Happify Health moved beyond CBT for depression to create programs spanning anxiety, stress, chronic illness support, and workplace wellbeing.

The trend is clear: patients expect more than one-off solutions. They want digital companions that can accompany them through various health challenges.

Gamification and Immersive Therapies

- If EndeavorRx® proved anything, it's that therapy doesn't have to feel like therapy. Gamification is becoming a central design philosophy.
- New DTx for chronic pain uses VR-based distraction therapy, immersing patients in calming, interactive worlds that reduce perceived pain.
- Pediatric programs are increasingly game-like, turning adherence into a form of play. A child who once resisted therapy logs in daily, not because they have to, but because they want to.

The insight is simple: engagement isn't a bonus—it's the medicine itself.

The Rise of Hybrid Therapies

Digital therapeutics are transitioning from standalone products to hybrid models that integrate human and digital support.

- Kaia Health integrates app-guided back pain exercises with live physiotherapist consultations.
- SilverCloud Health pairs digital CBT with therapist check-ins, ensuring patients get both scale and empathy.

The future lies in blending automation with human touch—personalized, scalable, and still deeply human.

Integration with Pharma Portfolios

Another trend is the strategic pairing of drugs and DTx.

- Sanofi bundles Happify's DTx with its mental health treatments, creating a two-pronged therapy.
- Roche explores MS monitoring tools as companions to its immunology drugs, transforming treatment from episodic injections to continuous care ecosystems.

For pharma, this isn't a side bet—it's differentiation in crowded markets.

Global Adoption and Regulation

Germany's DiGA Fast-Track has become a model for other regions, demonstrating how reimbursement can accelerate the adoption of digital health innovations. Other countries, from France to Japan, are exploring similar frameworks. Meanwhile, in emerging markets, mobile-first strategies are enabling leapfrogging: DTx delivered by SMS or lightweight apps where broadband is limited.

The future of DTx isn't Western-only—it's global.

The Lesson

Emerging trends indicate that digital therapeutics are maturing from novelty to necessity. They are:

Expanding from single-condition apps to multi-condition ecosystems.

- Leveraging gamification and VR to make therapy engaging.

- Blending digital programs with human support in hybrid models.
- Aligning with pharma portfolios for integrated care.
- Spreading globally as regulatory frameworks catch up.

Closing Thought

The early years of digital therapeutics were focused on proving their effectiveness. The coming years will be about proving they can scale, integrate, and endure. The emerging trend isn't just more apps—it's more medicine, reimagined: engaging, continuous, and global.

9.2 The Role of Genomics and Personalized Medicine

In 2003, when the Human Genome Project announced it had mapped all 3 billion letters of human DNA, the headlines promised a revolution. Medicine would soon be tailored to the individual, designed not for "the average patient" but for you. Two decades later, that promise is finally converging with digital therapeutics. The genome explains why patients respond differently to treatments; digital therapeutics can adapt in real time to how they live with those treatments.

Together, genomics and DTx point toward a future where therapy isn't just personalized—it's precisely engineered for the individual.

From Averages to Individuals

Traditional medicine is built on averages. A cholesterol-lowering drug is tested on thousands, then prescribed broadly. Yet two patients with the same prescription may respond very differently—because their genetic makeup is not the same.

Genomics uncovers these differences. Digital therapeutics operationalize them.

- A patient with a genetic predisposition to poor drug metabolism may need lower doses of medication. A digital companion app can monitor side effects, adjust behavioral interventions, and alert physicians in real time.
- A cancer patient's tumor may carry unique mutations. Genomic profiling guides drug choice, while a DTx supports adherence, tracks symptoms, and collects patient-reported outcomes between infusions.

The marriage of the molecular and the digital creates a care model that sees the whole person—genes and behaviors together.

Adaptive Therapy in Real Life

Personalized medicine is not just about choosing the right drug; it's about sustaining the right care.

- In diabetes, genomic insights may identify patients at higher risk of progression. A DTx like Omada Health can then provide tailored behavioral coaching, delivering more intensive interventions where the risk is greatest.

- In mental health, genetics may indicate a predisposition to certain conditions or responses to medication. Pairing that knowledge with adaptive CBT apps like Deprexis means therapy can be personalized both at the biological and behavioral level.

The result is medicine that doesn't just start right, but stays right as the patient's needs evolve.

Precision at Scale

Critics once argued that personalized medicine was too costly—sequencing genomes, tailoring drugs, customizing care. But digital therapeutics make precision scalable. Algorithms can deliver personalized modules to thousands at once, adapting therapy dynamically without requiring a clinician to intervene every time.

This is the paradox: the more digital therapeutics personalize, the more scalable they become.

The Lesson

The role of genomics and personalized medicine in digital therapeutics is to close the loop between:

- What patients need biologically (genetic profile, disease subtype).
- What patients need behaviorally (adherence, lifestyle support, symptom tracking).

Together, they shift medicine from "trial and error" to "tailored and adaptive."

Closing Thought

The future of digital therapeutics isn't just smart apps or clever algorithms. It's the fusion of two revolutions: genomics, which reveals the blueprint of the body, and digital therapeutics, which tailor care to the rhythms of daily life.

When combined, they promise something extraordinary: medicine that is not only personalized but personal—designed uniquely for you, responding uniquely to you, and evolving uniquely with you.

9.3 Global Expansion: Opportunities and Challenges in Emerging Markets

In a small town outside Bengaluru, a middle-aged man with Type 2 diabetes logs his meals into a smartphone app. The app, developed by an Indian health-tech start-up, sends him daily coaching messages in Kannada, his local language. It reminds him to take short walks after meals, provides culturally appropriate diet tips, and connects him with a remote health coach. For the first time, he feels supported in managing his disease—not by traveling to a distant clinic, but through the device in his pocket.

That story captures the promise of digital therapeutics in emerging markets: they can deliver quality care in places where doctors are scarce, infrastructure is limited, and chronic diseases are rising rapidly. But it also reveals the challenges: affordability, digital literacy, and regulatory frameworks are not yet keeping pace.

The Opportunity: Leapfrogging Traditional Barriers

Emerging markets often lack dense networks of hospitals or specialists. However, they do have one advantage: mobile penetration.

- In India, smartphone adoption exceeds 600 million users. This makes mobile-first DTx solutions, such as those for diabetes, hypertension, and mental health, scalable at the population level.
- In Africa, mobile health platforms already deliver medication reminders and maternal health tips via SMS. Extending these to full-fledged digital therapeutics is a natural progression.

Where traditional systems struggle to reach, digital therapeutics can leapfrog—offering access at scale, faster than brick-and-mortar expansion ever could.

Localization: Speaking the Patient's Language

Success in these markets requires more than technology—it requires cultural fit.

- A diet management app designed for the U.S. may emphasize low-carb diets. In India, where rice is a staple food, effective DTx adapts recommendations to local cuisine.

- Mental health programs must address stigma and integrate culturally relevant metaphors, as exemplified by the adaptation of SilverCloud Health for use in Asia and Africa.

Trust grows when patients see themselves reflected in the design.

The Challenge: Affordability and Reimbursement

However, promises meet resistance at the point of payment. Many emerging markets lack universal reimbursement frameworks, such as Germany's DiGA Fast-Track. Patients often pay out of pocket, limiting adoption.

- In Brazil, pilots of digital mental health platforms demonstrated strong outcomes but struggled with scaling up because insurers hesitated to cover the costs.
- In Nigeria, mobile diabetes programs have proven effective but faced drop-offs when patients were unable to sustain subscription fees.

Affordability remains the Achilles 'heel of global digital therapeutics (DTx) adoption.

The Regulatory Gap

Another barrier is the absence of clear regulatory frameworks. Without guidance, digital therapeutics risk being lumped in with wellness apps, undermining legitimacy.

- Japan and Singapore are emerging as leaders in building structured approval processes for digital therapeutics (DTx).
- In many other countries, regulation lags, leaving physicians and patients unsure whether these products can be trusted.

Until regulation catches up, adoption will remain fragmented.

The Lesson

Global expansion of digital therapeutics reveals both promise and paradox:

- Opportunity – leapfrogging weak infrastructure with mobile-first solutions.
- Strength – local adaptation that builds cultural trust.
- Challenge – affordability and reimbursement remain uneven.
- Gap – regulation needs to legitimize and standardize adoption.

The future of DTx in emerging markets isn't about exporting Western solutions—it's about building locally relevant, affordable, and trustworthy ecosystems.

Closing Thought

In emerging markets, digital therapeutics could democratize care on a scale the developed world never needed. The opportunity is breathtaking: millions gaining access to therapies that clinics and specialists could never reach. But realizing that vision will depend on solving the hardest problems—equity, cost, and trust.

Because the true test of digital therapeutics will not be whether they succeed in wealthy cities, but whether they can thrive in the small towns, rural villages, and underserved communities where the need is greatest.

9.4 The Evolving Relationship between Pharma, Tech Companies, and Healthcare Providers

In 2018, when Novartis partnered with Pear Therapeutics, the alliance raised eyebrows. Here was a century-old pharmaceutical giant working hand in hand with a start-up whose product wasn't a pill or device, but software for addiction therapy. At the same time, clinicians wondered, "Where do we fit into this picture?" If pharma and tech are developing therapies, do doctors prescribe them—or do they become part of the design process?

That tension—between old models and new roles—captures the evolving relationship at the heart of digital therapeutics. Pharma, tech, and providers are no longer operating in parallel. They are learning, sometimes awkwardly, to operate as a trio, each playing a role that the others cannot.

Pharma: Scale and Legitimacy

Pharmaceutical companies bring what start-ups often lack:

- Regulatory expertise.
- Distribution muscle.
- Established relationships with payers.

When Sanofi partnered with Happify Health, it wasn't just about mental health modules. It was about leveraging Sanofi's global infrastructure to bring Happify's DTx to millions of patients, transforming an app into a reimbursed, prescribable therapy. Pharma doesn't just scale—it legitimizes.

Tech Companies: Innovation and Agility

Tech companies bring speed, design, and user-centric thinking. They see patients not just as "cases" but as "users," and they know how to make therapy engaging.

- Kaia Health turned smartphone cameras into motion coaches, blending AI with physical therapy exercises.
- Woebot Health built an empathetic chatbot that adapts in real time to patient mood—a feat of user experience design that pharma would struggle to build an empathetic chatbot that adapts in real-time to a patient'sggle to build internally.

Where pharma provides reach, tech provides freshness. Together, they create therapies that are both credible and compelling.

Providers: Trust and Clinical Integration

And yet, none of this works without healthcare providers. Patients still look to their doctors for validation: Is this real? Should I use it? Providers are the gatekeepers of trust.

- In Germany's DiGA program, adoption accelerated once doctors began prescribing DTx directly. Patients felt safe because the recommendation came from a trusted clinician.
- In the U.S., Propeller Health succeeded because pulmonologists could see inhaler data directly in dashboards—integrated into their workflow, not bolted on as an extra burden.

Providers ensure DTx are not just apps patients try, but therapies patients sustain.

From Silos to Ecosystems

Historically, pharma, tech, and providers lived in silos:

- Pharma made drugs.
- Tech built tools.
- Providers delivered care.

Digital therapeutics collapse those boundaries. Success depends on ecosystem thinking:

- Pharma provides legitimacy and reimbursement pathways.
- Tech provides design and adaptability.
- Providers provide trust and clinical oversight.

It is not a handoff. It is a handshake.

The Lesson

The evolving relationship among pharma, tech, and providers is not about replacing roles. It is about redefining them.

- Pharma shifts from pill-maker to outcome-partner.
- Tech shifts from app-maker to healthcare innovator.

- Providers shift from prescribers to co-pilots of digital care.

Together, they are building a new model where care is continuous, connected, and collaborative.

Closing Thought

The story of digital therapeutics is not just about technology. It's about relationships—between industries that once eyed each other warily, and between patients and the systems that serve them.

In the end, the partnerships that thrive will be the ones that recognize this simple truth: no single player can make digital therapeutics succeed alone. The future will belong to those who collaborate—not as rivals protecting turf, but as allies building a new kind of medicine.

9.5 Predictions for the Next Decade: What Lies Ahead for Digital Therapeutics

On a winter morning in 2033, a woman with heart failure wakes up to her smartwatch gently vibrating. Overnight, it has tracked subtle changes in her heart rate variability and oxygen saturation. Her digital therapeutic has already flagged the risk of early decompensation. Before she even makes her morning coffee, her physician has reviewed the alert and adjusted her treatment plan remotely. No ER visit. No hospitalization. Care delivered before the crisis.

This scene is not science fiction—it is the trajectory digital therapeutics are already tracing. The next decade will determine whether this vision becomes mainstream medicine or remains a collection of promising but fragmented experiments.

From Adjuncts to First-Line Therapies

Today, digital therapeutics are often framed as "adjuncts"—tools to support drugs or fill gaps between appointments. In the next decade, some will stand alone as first-line interventions.

- Mental health DTx, like Deprexis or Woebot Health, may become standard starting points before medication is considered.
- Lifestyle-focused DTx, such as Omada Health, could be prescribed at the earliest signs of metabolic risk, reshaping prevention.

The line between "digital" and "traditional" therapy will blur—patients may encounter digital first, drugs second.

Hyper-Personalization at Scale

Artificial intelligence and genomics will fuse with DTx, creating therapies that are not just tailored to patient subgroups but to individuals.

- A cancer patient's genomic profile will guide drug selection, while a DTx monitors side effects and adjusts behavioral support in real time.
- An insomnia app like Somryst® won't just deliver CBT-I modules—it will adjust nightly routines based on biometric data from wearables.

The future is not one-size-fits-all therapy but one-of-one therapy—personalized at genetic, behavioral, and environmental levels.

Integration into Healthcare Systems

By 2035, successful health systems will not treat DTx as add-ons but as infrastructure.

- In Germany, where the DiGA Fast-Track already sets the pace, DTx will be embedded in every prescription pathway.
- In the U.S., payer models will catch up—linking reimbursement to real-world evidence, much like value-based care for drugs today.

The expectation will shift: prescribing a drug without a digital companion may seem incomplete.

Global Expansion with Local Flavor

Emerging markets will become proving grounds for scale.

- In India and Africa, mobile-first ecosystems will make DTx the default care model in rural areas where specialists are scarce.
- Programs will succeed not by exporting Western designs but by tailoring to local languages, diets, and cultural contexts.

The global story of DTx will not be one of uniformity, but of localization.

The Pharma–Tech–Provider Convergence

In the next decade, the uneasy partnerships of today will mature into true ecosystems.

- Pharma will provide clinical rigor and market access.
- Tech companies will deliver adaptive, engaging design.
- Providers will remain the trusted human face of care, empowered by continuous data from DTx.

Together, they will shift the definition of healthcare from episodic treatment to continuous management.

The Lesson

The next decade will see digital therapeutics evolve in five key ways:

1. From adjuncts to frontline therapies.
2. From averages to hyper-personalized care.
3. From pilots to system-wide infrastructure.

4. From Western innovation to global adoption.
5. From fragmented industries to integrated ecosystems.

The trajectory is set—but the pace will depend on how quickly trust, reimbursement, and regulation keep up.

Closing Thought

In the 2010s, digital therapeutics were novelties. In the 2020s, they became experiments with regulatory approval. By the 2030s, they may be as routine as pills and stethoscopes.

The real question is not whether digital therapeutics will succeed—it is whether healthcare systems, payers, and patients can adapt fast enough to embrace a world where code doesn't just support medicine. Code is medicine.

And when that shift becomes ordinary, we may look back on today's apps and sensors the way we now look at early antibiotics: crude beginnings of a revolution that changed everything.

Chapter 10

Conclusion

In 2017, when the FDA approved reSET®, the first prescription digital therapeutic, it felt like a footnote in medical history. A small app for substance use disorder, backed by clinical trials, quietly entered the official canon of medicine. Many dismissed it as a curiosity. Pills were real. Injections were real. Could software ever truly be medicine?

Fast forward a decade, and the landscape looks very different. From insomnia to ADHD, from diabetes to chronic pain, digital therapeutics have proven not only that they can work—but that they can change the very rhythm of care. They have shifted medicine from something episodic, reactive, and confined to clinics into something continuous, proactive, and woven into daily life.

The Promise Realized

Throughout this book, we've traced how digital therapeutics emerged, battled skepticism, navigated regulation, and began to scale. Their promise is now undeniable:

- For patients, they offer personalized, always-on therapy that adapts to their lives.
- For providers, they extend care between appointments, supplying data and insights once invisible.
- For payers, they hold the potential to cut costs by preventing crises before they happen.
- For pharma, they represent not a threat but an evolution—expanding from drugmakers to health outcome partners.

The story of digital therapeutics is not about replacing medicine. It is about completing it.

Strategic Imperatives for Pharma

For pharmaceutical companies, the lesson is clear: standing still is not an option. The companies that thrive will be those that:

1. Invest in digital therapeutics as companions and stand-alone interventions.
2. Build partnerships with nimble tech start-ups while bringing scale and legitimacy.
3. Redefine success not only in terms of prescriptions filled, but outcomes achieved.

The opportunity is not just commercial—it is existential. Pharma has the chance to lead the fusion of biology and digital, shaping the future of healthcare itself.

A Vision for the Future of Healthcare

The stethoscope, when first introduced in the 19th century, was met with skepticism. Doctors preferred listening with the naked ear. Today, no physician practices without one. Digital therapeutics are at the same inflection point. One day, prescribing a drug without a digital companion may feel as incomplete as diagnosing without a stethoscope.

The future is medicine that is:

- Personalized—tailored to genes, behaviors, and context.
- Continuous—living with patients, not just in clinics.
- Collaborative—where pharma, tech, and providers build ecosystems together.
- Trusted—with privacy, ethics, and equity as non-negotiable foundations.

Closing Thought

When historians write about this moment in healthcare, they may not describe it as the age of apps or wearables. They may describe it as the moment medicine stopped being bound by the clinic and began traveling with the patient—into homes, into pockets, into daily routines.

The code to cure was never about replacing the pill. It was about unlocking a new way of healing—where medicine is no longer something we take, but something we live.

10.1 Recap: The Potential for Digital Therapeutics in Pharma Marketing

When Propeller Health first attached sensors to inhalers, pharmaceutical marketers barely took notice. It seemed like a niche gadget, useful for a subset of asthma patients but hardly transformative. Then the data began to flow—millions of puffs tracked, adherence rates mapped, and environmental triggers identified. Suddenly, inhalers were no longer just commodities. They were data-generating platforms, opening new ways for pharma to demonstrate value, engage patients, and even negotiate with payers.

That moment revealed the larger story: digital therapeutics are not just clinical innovations. They are also marketing revolutions. They redefine how pharma companies connect with patients, physicians, and payers—not through brochures or brand campaigns, but through measurable outcomes and lived experiences.

Beyond the Pill: Pharma as Partner in Care

For decades, pharma's role was largely transactional—developing drugs, promoting them, and persuading prescribers. Digital therapeutics change the equation.

- By pairing a DTx with a drug, pharma shifts from selling a product to delivering a solution. A depression treatment bundled with a CBT-based DTx is no longer just serotonin regulation—it's a comprehensive mental health ecosystem.
- With tools like Kaia Health, pharma can support chronic pain patients not just at the point of prescription, but throughout their therapy journey, reinforcing adherence and demonstrating commitment to outcomes.

The marketing story is no longer about features. It's about outcomes that patients and payers can see.

Data as Differentiator

In crowded therapeutic categories, differentiation can be challenging. Digital therapeutics offer a new lever: data.

- Propeller's inhaler data didn't just improve adherence—it gave pharma real-world evidence to show payers that their drugs delivered sustained value.
- Omada Health's diabetes prevention results enabled pharma partners to approach insurers not with promotional claims, but with hard numbers: fewer hospitalizations and lower long-term costs.

For pharma marketers, this turns conversations with stakeholders from persuasion into proof.

Patient Engagement as a Marketing Asset

Pharma has long struggled with patient engagement once prescriptions are filled. DTx solves that gap.

- Patients using EndeavorRx or Somryst interact with the therapy daily. Every touchpoint becomes an opportunity to reinforce adherence, capture feedback, and sustain connection.
- Unlike traditional campaigns, which often end at the prescription pad, digital therapeutics keep the brand alive in the patient's daily life, creating trust and loyalty.

This is marketing, not as messaging, but as experience design.

The Lesson

The potential for digital therapeutics in pharma marketing can be summed up in three shifts:

1. From product to solution – drugs bundled with digital therapeutics (DTx) deliver holistic care.
2. From persuasion to proof – outcomes data replaces promotional claims.
3. From episodic to continuous engagement – brands live with patients, not just in clinics.

For the pharmaceutical industry, this is more than just innovation. It is reinvention.

Closing Thought

Pharma marketing once revolved around slogans and samples. In the era of digital therapeutics, it will revolve around something more powerful: outcomes experienced and measured in real time.

The potential here is profound. Pharma companies that embrace DTx are not just marketing medicines—they are marketing trust, data, and continuity of care. And in a healthcare world defined by skepticism, those may be the most valuable assets of all.

10.2 Strategic Imperatives for Pharma Companies

In 2018, Roche made a quiet move that would ripple through the industry: it invested in digital platforms for multiple sclerosis (MS), not as a side project but as a core companion to its blockbuster drugs. Instead of limiting its role to selling medication, Roche positioned itself as a partner in disease management. Patients weren't just receiving infusions—they were enrolled in continuous monitoring programs, where digital tools tracked symptoms, captured relapses early, and guided lifestyle adjustments.

The lesson was clear: digital therapeutics aren't just an add-on. They are strategic. For pharma, the question is no longer if they should invest in DTx, but how they must embed it into their business models.

1. **Move from Product-Centric to Outcome-Centric Thinking**

   Pharma has long focused on the molecule as the hero. In the DTx era, the hero is the outcome.

   - Bundling antidepressants with digital CBT creates an ecosystem that addresses both neurochemistry and behavior.
   - Combining COPD medications with Propeller Health's inhaler sensors doesn't just sell more drugs—it demonstrates reduced ER visits, proving value to payers.

   Strategic imperative: Shift from "selling drugs" to delivering outcomes.

2. **Build Partnerships, Don't Go it Alone**

   Pharma excels at regulation, scale, and payer access. Tech excels at agility, design, and data science. The companies that thrive will marry these strengths.

   - Novartis and Pear Therapeutics pioneered this model, even if their partnership ended, showing both the promise and pitfalls of collaboration.
   - Sanofi and Happify Health proved that combining pharma's reach with tech's innovation could expand mental health offerings far beyond pills.

   Strategic imperative: Cultivate symbiotic partnerships with digital health innovators rather than trying to build everything in-house.

3. **Integrate DTx into the Commercial Model:** Digital therapeutics must be more than side projects. They should be woven into brand strategies, sales narratives, and market access plans.
    - In Germany, DTx listed in the DiGA registry are prescribed and reimbursed alongside drugs. Pharma companies there have learned to market therapy bundles as standard of care, not novelties.
    - In the U.S., some pharmaceutical sales representatives now promote drug–digital therapy (DTx) combinations, giving physicians not just a pill to prescribe but a digital program to extend its impact.

    Strategic imperative: Make DTx part of the core commercial offering, not a bolt-on experiment.
4. **Leverage Data as a Differentiator:** Every digital therapeutic generates a stream of real-world evidence, including usage patterns, outcomes, and adherence metrics. Pharma can harness this data to:
    - Strengthen reimbursement negotiations with payers.
    - Differentiate brands in crowded categories.
    - Shape clinical trial designs with continuous patient-reported outcomes.

    Strategic imperative: Treat data not as exhaust, but as currency.
5. **Redefine the Relationship with Patients:** Pharma has always struggled to engage patients directly. Digital therapeutics open a door.
    - With EndeavorRx®, families interact daily with a therapy that has pharma's backing.
    - With Omada Health, patients receive coaching and feedback that reflect the brand's ongoing role in their well-being.

    Strategic imperative: Shift from episodic contact to continuous, trust-based engagement with patients.

The Lesson

Pharma companies cannot approach digital therapeutics as experiments on the side of the business. They are imperatives that demand:

1. Outcome-centric strategies.

2. Bold partnerships.
3. Commercial integration.
4. Data-driven differentiation.
5. Direct patient engagement.

Closing Thought

The pharmaceutical industry has reinvented itself before—embracing biotechnology, adapting to generics, and navigating regulatory upheavals. Digital therapeutics represent the next reinvention.

The companies that act decisively will not just sell more drugs. They will redefine themselves as health outcome companies, competing not on pill counts but on patient lives improved. And in that shift lies the future of pharma's relevance—and resilience—in the digital age.

10.3 Final Thoughts: A Vision for the Future of Healthcare

In the spring of 2030, a young woman in Nairobi wakes up to a gentle vibration on her wrist. Her wearable device has detected changes in her heart rhythm and prompts her to consult her doctor. Within minutes, she is on a telemedicine call. Her physician has already received her biometric data and prescribes not only medication but also a digital therapeutic tailored to her stress patterns. The app delivers breathing exercises in her language, tracks adherence, and adapts daily. What once required multiple clinic visits now happens in the flow of her morning.

This is the healthcare future digital therapeutics point toward: personalized, proactive, and present in daily life.

From Episodic to Continuous Care

Traditional medicine has always been episodic—visit a doctor, get a prescription, wait until the next flare-up. Digital therapeutics transform this into a continuous loop of care, where therapy lives with the patient, adapts in real-time, and prevents crises before they occur.

The shift is profound:

- Drugs treat biology.
- Digital therapeutics guide behavior.
- Together, they create whole-person medicine.

From Marketing to Meaning

For the pharmaceutical industry, the implications extend beyond product promotion. The future of healthcare marketing won't be about glossy brochures or physician detailing. It will be about demonstrating value in real time—showing patients, providers, and payers that therapies improve lives measurably, sustainably, and equitably.

Every inhaler puff tracked, every insomnia night shortened, every ADHD child's attention span improved—these aren't just outcomes. They are proof points in the new language of trust.

From Access to Equity

The promise of digital therapeutics should not be limited to wealthy urban centers. The true test will be whether they reach underserved populations in rural India, sub-Saharan Africa, or marginalized communities in the West.

Affordable, localized, and culturally relevant digital therapeutics (DTx) could finally close long-standing care gaps. If code can travel where doctors cannot, healthcare can begin to fulfill its oldest promise: to care for all, not just some.

The Lesson

The vision for the future of healthcare is not technology for its own sake. It is technology in the service of humanity:

- Care that adapts to the patient, not the other way around.
- Systems that measure success not by revenue, but by lives improved.
- Partnerships between pharma, tech, and providers that build ecosystems rather than empires.

Closing Thought

When historians look back on this era, they may see digital therapeutics as the quiet catalyst that redefined medicine. Not as replacements for drugs, but as companions—pieces of code that learned, nudged, and adapted, turning treatment into something patients lived with, not waited for.

The vision is simple but radical: a healthcare system where medicine is no longer episodic intervention but continuous partnership. Where every patient carries, not just a prescription, but a digital ally. And where healing is not delivered only in clinics and hospitals, but in the rhythms of everyday life.

The code to cure was never just about software. It was about rewriting the story of healthcare itself—from a system that reacts to sickness, to one that anticipates, prevents, and sustains wellness.

Appendix A

Glossary of Key Terms

Every revolution invents its own vocabulary. When railroads transformed commerce, words like junction, freight, and time zone became part of daily life. When the internet reshaped communication, we learned about email, browsers, and logins. Digital therapeutics is no different. To understand its potential—and to communicate effectively with regulators, payers, or patients—you need to be fluent in its terminology.

This glossary is more than a dictionary. It is a decoder ring—translating the language of algorithms, clinical trials, and market access into concepts that marketers, clinicians, and innovators can actually understand and utilize.

Glossary of Key Terms

A

Adherence: The degree to which a patient follows prescribed therapy (medication, digital program, or both). In DTx, adherence is measurable in real-time through app logins, completed sessions, or sensor data.

AI (Artificial Intelligence): Computer systems that simulate human intelligence to analyze data, recognize patterns, and adapt interventions. Key in personalizing digital therapeutics.

Algorithm: A set of rules or calculations used by digital therapeutics to deliver interventions, track behaviors, or adjust therapy dynamically.

B

Blockchain: A secure, distributed ledger technology that ensures data privacy, traceability, and integrity. Increasingly used in healthcare for managing sensitive patient data in digital therapeutics (DTx).

Brand Differentiation: Marketing strategy to distinguish a product from competitors. In DTx, differentiation often comes from outcomes data, personalization, or integration with drugs.

C

CE Marking: A certification mark that indicates a product's conformity with European health, safety, and performance standards, mandatory for DTx sold in the EU.

Chronic Disease Management: Coordinated healthcare interventions and self-management support for chronic conditions, such as diabetes, COPD, or hypertension—areas where digital therapeutics (DTx) thrives.

Clinical Validation: Evidence generated through trials or real-world studies demonstrating that a DTx produces meaningful health outcomes.

Compliance: Patient's fulfillment of prescribed therapy. Often used interchangeably with adherence, but in DTx, it emphasizes both the frequency and quality of use.

D

Data Privacy: Legal and ethical framework ensuring protection of patient health data collected by digital therapeutics. Governed by laws such as HIPAA (U.S.) and GDPR (EU).

Deprexis: A digital cognitive behavioral therapy (CBT) program for depression, one of the earliest validated DTx in Europe.

DiGA (Digitale Gesundheitsanwendungen): Germany's "Fast-Track" program for digital health applications, allowing DTx to be prescribed by doctors and reimbursed by statutory health insurance.

Digital Biomarker: Physiological or behavioral data collected digitally (e.g., step counts, heart rate variability) used to diagnose, monitor, or predict health outcomes.

Digital Therapeutics (DTx): Evidence-based, clinically validated software interventions designed to prevent, manage, or treat medical conditions.

E

Engagement Metrics: Measurements of how often and how deeply patients interact with a DTx (e.g., number of sessions, time spent, tasks completed).

EndeavorRx®: The first FDA-approved video game therapeutic, developed by Akili Interactive, to treat pediatric ADHD.

Epidemiology-Based Forecasting: Use of population-level disease data to predict demand for drugs or DTx interventions.

F

FDA (Food and Drug Administration): U.S. regulatory body responsible for approving and monitoring drugs, devices, and digital therapeutics.

Fast Track (Regulatory): An accelerated regulatory process used in some markets (e.g., Germany's DiGA) to bring DTx quickly to patients.

G

Gamification: Use of game-like elements in non-game contexts, widely applied in DTx to improve adherence and engagement.

GDPR (General Data Protection Regulation): EU regulation governing data protection and privacy, critical for DTx companies handling patient data.

Generics (in the context of DTx): While usually referring to off-patent drugs, in digital therapeutics, it refers to the possibility of commoditizing basic software-based interventions.

H

Hybrid Care: A model combining digital therapeutics with traditional in-person therapy, often seen in mental health applications like SilverCloud Health.

HIPAA (Health Insurance Portability and Accountability Act): U.S. law protecting patient health information.

I

Integration (DTx + Pharma): The process of aligning digital therapeutics with pharmaceutical brands, often through co-packaging, co-prescribing, or companion apps.

Interoperability: Ability of DTx systems to exchange data with electronic health records (EHRs), wearables, or provider platforms.

J

Journey Mapping (Patient Journey): Mapping the touchpoints a patient encounters during diagnosis, treatment, and care—key to identifying where Digital Therapeutics (DTx) can intervene.

K

Key Performance Indicators (KPIs): Specific, measurable goals used to track the success of DTx—ranging from adherence rates to hospitalization reduction.

L

Lifecycle Management (Brand Lifecycle): Pharma strategy to extend the commercial life of a drug. With DTx, the lifecycle can expand through digital adjuncts and companion solutions.

Log-In Frequency: A proxy for adherence in DTx, measuring how often patients use the therapy.

M

Machine Learning (ML): A subset of AI that uses data to improve the performance of algorithms without explicit programming, often applied in predictive analytics in DTx.

Market Access: The process of ensuring that therapies (drugs or DTx) reach patients by securing reimbursement and inclusion in care pathways.

MHLW (Ministry of Health, Labour and Welfare, Japan): Japanese regulatory authority that approved CureApp's smoking cessation DTx.

N

NICE (National Institute for Health and Care Excellence): U.K. health authority responsible for evaluating cost-effectiveness and clinical utility of therapies, including DTx.

Novel Endpoint: A new way of measuring therapeutic effect, often made possible by DTx (e.g., changes in sleep quality tracked by wearables).

O

Omada Health: A digital therapeutics company focused on diabetes prevention and chronic disease management.

Outcomes-Based Marketing: A strategy that emphasizes proven patient outcomes (rather than features) as the core of brand messaging.

P

Patient-Centricity: Designing therapies—including DTx—around the needs, preferences, and behaviors of patients.

Payer: Organizations (public or private insurers) responsible for covering therapy costs. Payers are key gatekeepers for the adoption of digital therapeutics (DTx).

Propeller Health: Company providing inhaler sensors and analytics for asthma and COPD management.

Q

Quality of Life (QoL): A broad measure of health outcomes that extends beyond symptom reduction and is increasingly central to DTx value propositions.

R

Real-World Evidence (RWE): Clinical and economic outcomes data collected outside controlled trials, critical for payer negotiations in DTx.

Reimbursement Pathways: Regulatory and payer processes that determine whether DTx are covered financially, e.g., Germany's DiGA.

Remote Monitoring: Continuous patient health tracking outside clinical settings, often enabled by wearables and integrated DTx.

S

SaMD (Software as a Medical Device): Regulatory category for software that performs medical functions without being part of hardware.

Scaling: Expanding a DTx from pilot trials to broad patient adoption, requiring marketing, partnerships, and reimbursement.

SilverCloud Health: A digital platform offering evidence-based mental health interventions, widely adopted in the U.K. NHS.

T

Telemedicine: Delivery of healthcare remotely, often integrated with DTx to provide holistic virtual care.

Therapeutic Alliance: The relationship between patient and provider; DTx are increasingly measured on their ability to support or extend this bond.

U

Unmet Need: Healthcare gaps not adequately addressed by existing treatments—prime targets for digital therapeutics (DTx) innovation.

User Experience (UX): Design and usability aspects of a digital therapeutic, critical to ensuring adherence and patient satisfaction.

V

Value Demonstration: The process of showing evidence of clinical, economic, and patient-centered benefits of DTx to stakeholders.

Virtual Reality (VR) Therapeutics: Immersive, software-based therapies treating conditions like PTSD, anxiety, and chronic pain.

W

Wellness App: Consumer-facing health applications for lifestyle improvement (e.g., meditation, fitness). Distinguished from DTx by lack of clinical validation and regulatory approval.

Wearable: Devices (smartwatches, sensors) that track health parameters, often integrated with DTx for remote monitoring.

X–Z

XR (Extended Reality) Therapies: A combination of AR/VR-based digital interventions for psychiatric and neurological conditions.

Z-Score (Clinical Analytics): A statistical measure used in some DTx studies to assess baseline versus intervention outcomes.

This glossary not only defines terms but also anchors them in the DTx–pharma marketing context, so that brand managers, students, and executives can immediately see relevance.

Appendix B

List of Digital Therapeutics and their Applications

In 2017, when reSET® became the first FDA-approved prescription digital therapeutic for substance use disorder, the approval felt almost symbolic. Few outside the industry noticed. But that small moment became the opening chapter of a much larger story. Since then, digital therapeutics have proliferated across conditions—from insomnia to ADHD, from diabetes to COPD. Each new approval is not just a product launch; it's another proof point that software can heal.

This appendix collects the most important examples of digital therapeutics to date. Think of it as a field guide: a way to understand not only what exists, but also what's possible.

Notable Digital Therapeutics and Their Applications

1. **reSET® (Pear Therapeutics, U.S.)**

   Condition: Substance use disorder

   Application: Provides cognitive behavioral therapy modules to support patients in recovery. FDA-cleared.

   Lesson: The trailblazer—proof that digital therapeutics could enter regulatory frameworks once reserved for drugs.

2. **reSET-O® (Pear Therapeutics, U.S.)**

   Condition: Opioid use disorder

   Application: Designed to be used alongside buprenorphine and clinician supervision.

   Lesson: One of the first "companion" DTx, showing how digital and pharmacological therapies can reinforce one another.

3. **Somryst® (Pear Therapeutics, U.S.)**

   Condition: Chronic insomnia

Application: Delivers digital cognitive behavioral therapy for insomnia (CBT-I).

Lesson: Software as a frontline treatment for conditions where drugs were once the default.

4. **EndeavorRx® (Akili Interactive, U.S.)**

   Condition: Pediatric ADHD

   Application: A video game that improves attention function in children aged 8–12.

   Lesson: Gamification as medicine—changing not only outcomes but perceptions of what therapy can look like.

5. **Propeller Health (U.S.)**

   Condition: Asthma, COPD

   Application: Sensors attached to inhalers track use and environmental triggers, feeding real-time data to patients and clinicians.

   Lesson: Adherence and prevention—medicine that anticipates crises before they occur.

6. **Kaia Health (Germany/U.S.)**

   Condition: Chronic back pain, COPD

   Application: AI-powered motion tracking and personalized exercise programs delivered via smartphone.

   Lesson: Physiotherapy scaled through digital coaching, bridging shortages of human providers.

7. **Omada Health (U.S.)**

   Condition: Diabetes prevention, obesity, hypertension, behavioral health

   Application: Digital coaching and behavioral modification programs to prevent chronic disease progression.

   Lesson: The pioneer of "lifestyle medicine as a service," backed by real-world evidence convincing payers to reimburse.

8. **Deprexis (Germany, Servier)**

   Condition: Depression

   Application: Online CBT-based program, widely used in Europe.

Lesson: A digital bridge where access to therapists is limited, extending care to underserved populations.

9. **SilverCloud Health (U.K./U.S.)**

   Condition: Depression, anxiety, chronic illness support

   Application: Digital CBT modules, often combined with therapist support.

   Lesson: The hybridmodel—balancing scale with human empathy.

10. **Happify Health (U.S.)**

   Condition: Stress, anxiety, chronic disease support

   Application: Gamified CBT and mindfulness exercises, now partnered with pharma for broader therapeutic uses.

   Lesson: Expanding mental health care through engaging, scalable tools.

The Bigger Picture

Taken together, these digital therapeutics reveal a pattern:

- They start in areas of unmet need (mental health, insomnia, chronic conditions).
- They succeed when they combine clinical rigor with patient engagement.
- They thrive when they partner with pharma or align with reimbursement models.

Closing Thought

This appendix isn't just a list—it's a map of a revolution in progress. Each entry is a case study in possibility, and together they tell us where digital therapeutics have been, where they are heading, and why they are no longer a novelty.

Because when software stops being an accessory and becomes the therapy itself, every new product is more than a launch. It's another signal that the future of medicine is being rewritten—one app, one algorithm, one patient at a time.

Appendix B: List of Digital Therapeutics and Their Applications

Condition / Therapy Area	Product	Company	Regulatory Status	Marketing Implications
Substance Use Disorder	reSET®	Pear Therapeutics (U.S.)	FDA-cleared (2017)	First FDA-approved DTx; Positioned pharma as partner in behavioral interventions; proved DTx could meet regulatory rigor.
Opioid Use Disorder	reSET-O®	Pear Therapeutics (U.S.)	FDA-cleared (2017)	Demonstrated drug-DTx synergy; used with buprenorphine to improve adherence and outcomes; opens new value-based contracting opportunities.
Chronic Insomnia	Somryst®	Pear Therapeutics (U.S.)	FDA-cleared (2020)	First prescription DTx for insomnia; provides a non-drug alternative; strong payer relevance where sleep medications face reimbursement pressure.
ADHD (Pediatric)	EndeavorRx®	Akili Interactive (U.S.)	FDA-cleared (2020)	World's first video game therapy; unique engagement model; reshpaes patient and caregiver perceptions of what "medicine" looks like.
Asthma (COPD)	Propeller Health	Propeller Health (U.S.)	FDA 510(k) cleared devices	Enhances inhaler adherence; creates real-world datasets; strengthens payer negotiations by demonstrating reduced ER visits.
Chronic Back Pain / COPD	Kaia Health	Kaia Health (Germany / U.S.); CE-marked in EU	FDA breakthrough designation; AI-driven physical therapy	Scales scarce physiotherapy resources; supports Pharma's move into non-drug interventions.

Contd...

Condition / Therapy Area	Product	Company	Regulatory Status	Marketing Implications
Diabetes Prevention / Chronic Conditions	Omada Health	Omada Health (U.S.)	Covered by multiple payers; validated by RWE Early proof of payer adoption	Real-world cost-savings data strengthens pharma partnerships and payer negotiations.
Depression	Deprexis	Servier (Germany)	CE-marked in the EU; widely adopted in Europe	One of the most established DTx; legitimizes digital CBT; bridges gaps in therapy access where clinicians are scarce.
Mental Health / Chronic Illness Support	SilverCloud Health	SilverCloud (U.K./U.S.)	CE-marked; adopted in NHS & U.S. systems	Hyrbrid care model; supports scale while keeping clinician trust; strong case for pharma bundling with psyhiatric medications
Mental Health / Behavioral Support	Happify Health	Happify Health (U.S.)	CE-marked; partnerships with pharma	Gamified, engaging modules; attractive to pharma brands seeking differeentiation in crowded therapeutic areas.

- This snapshot shows how DTx has carved its niches:
- Regulatory legitimacy (FDA/CE/DiGA) is the gateway to adoption.
- Payer alignment is the make-or-break for scale.
- Pharma partnerships transform DTx from stand-alone tools into integrated therapeutic ecosystems.

Closing Thought

This appendix is not just a catalogue—it's a playbook. Each row shows a way pharma can learn, partner, and expand: from drug–DTx bundles to standalone digital products that redefine engagement. The marketing implication is clear: pharma is no longer selling molecules alone. It is selling outcomes, powered by code.

Appendix C

Regulatory Resources and Guidelines

When Pear Therapeutics won FDA clearance for reSET®, it wasn't just a milestone for one company—it was a milestone for medicine itself. Regulators, long accustomed to reviewing molecules and devices, had to ask a new question: How do you regulate a therapy made of code?

That moment set in motion a global rethinking of healthcare oversight. Today, regulatory bodies from Washington to Berlin to Tokyo are writing new playbooks—deciding how to evaluate, approve, and reimburse digital therapeutics. For pharma marketers, understanding these frameworks is not optional. It is the difference between an experiment that stalls and a product that scales.

This appendix compiles the key regulatory resources that shape the digital therapeutic (DTx) landscape.

United States: Food and Drug Administration (FDA)

Framework: DTx are typically regulated under the Software as a Medical Device (SaMD) category.

Pathways:

- De Novo classification for novel products (e.g., reSET®).
- 510(k) clearance if a predicate device exists (e.g., some inhaler sensors).

Key Guidance: FDA's "Digital Health Innovation Action Plan" and SaMD guidance documents.

Implication for Pharma: FDA clearance provides legitimacy but requires rigorous clinical evidence. Marketers can leverage this as proof of efficacy to payers and providers.

European Union: European Medicines Agency (EMA) and National Agencies

Framework: DTx falls under the Medical Device Regulation (MDR) framework as SaMD.

CE Marking: Required for commercialization across EU states. Indicates conformity to safety, performance, and quality standards.

Key Guidance: EU MDR documents; EMA's digital health initiatives.

Implication for Pharma: CE Marking is crucial for gaining access to the EU market. Marketing must emphasize compliance and evidence to reassure both clinicians and patients.

Germany: DiGA Fast-Track (Digitale Gesundheitsanwendungen)

Framework: World's first structured reimbursement pathway for DTx.

Process

Companies apply to the BfArM (Bundesinstitut für Arzneimittel und Medizinprodukte, or Federal Institute for Drugs and Medical Devices).

Must demonstrate positive healthcare effects (clinical or structural).

Products are listed in the official DiGA Directory and reimbursed by insurers.

Key Guidance: BfArM's DiGA guidelines and checklists.

Implication for Pharma: Germany is the blueprint. DTx can be prescribed like drugs. Pharma marketers should look to DiGA as a model for payer engagement worldwide.

Japan: Ministry of Health, Labour and Welfare (MHLW)

Framework: Emerging pathway for DTx, particularly in chronic disease and mental health.

Notable Example: In 2020, Japan approved a smoking cessation digital therapeutic (DTx) app developed by CureApp.

Implication for Pharma: Japan is positioning itself as a leader in Asia; partnerships here may set precedents across the region.

Other Markets (Highlights)

- **U.K. (NICE):** Evaluating DTx under its Evidence Standards Framework for Digital Health.
- **France**: Moving toward DiGA-like frameworks for reimbursement of digital medical devices.
- **Canada**: Health Canada regulates Digital Therapeutics (DTx) under the guidance of SaMD, aligning with FDA/EMA principles.
- **Singapore**: Health Sciences Authority (HSA) is piloting regulatory sandboxes for digital health.

Regulatory frameworks are not just hurdles. They are marketing assets. Approval, CE marking, or DiGA listing signal legitimacy to patients, providers, and payers. The companies that succeed will not treat regulation as an obstacle, but as proof—woven directly into their value story.

Closing Thought

Every new therapeutic revolution forces regulators to adapt. Just as antibiotics required new safety standards in the 20th century, digital therapeutics are forcing agencies to rethink what "medicine" means in the 21st.

For pharmaceutical marketers, the message is simple: understand these frameworks, speak their language, and utilize them as a bridge to build trust. Because in the world of digital therapeutics, regulatory approval is not just a license to sell—it is a license to believe.

Appendix D

Case Studies and Success Stories

Every revolution is best understood not through theory but through stories. Antibiotics became real when penicillin saved wounded soldiers in World War II. The internet became real when email replaced letters. Digital therapeutics become real when we see how they change individual lives—and entire systems.

This appendix compiles some of the most compelling stories of digital therapeutics in action, illustrating how companies have overcome skepticism, demonstrated value, and transformed patient journeys.

Case Study 1: Pear Therapeutics and reSET® – Breaking Ground in Addiction Care

Background

Substance use disorder (SUD) affects millions globally. Traditional therapies—counseling, group therapy, and pharmacological support—are effective but plagued by high relapse rates, limited access to specialists, and social stigma. By 2017, the U.S. opioid epidemic had pushed regulators, payers, and providers to look urgently for scalable, evidence-based solutions.

Challenge

Patients needed tools to reinforce therapy outside the clinic. Providers lacked visibility into adherence and progress between visits. And most importantly, regulators had no precedent for approving a software-only therapeutic. Could code, on its own, ever be validated as medicine?

Intervention

Pear Therapeutics developed reSET®, a prescription digital therapeutic delivering cognitive behavioral therapy (CBT) modules via smartphone. Unlike wellness apps, reSET underwent randomized controlled trials (RCTs) and the FDA's De Novo pathway. It wasn't just designed as a supplement—it was positioned as a bona fide therapeutic intervention.

- Patients engaged with structured CBT lessons.
- Clinicians received dashboards tracking progress.
- The system reinforced abstinence behaviors, providing support between therapy sessions.

Outcome

- FDA clearance in 2017—the first prescription DTx approval in the U.S.
- Clinical trials showed improved abstinence rates compared to control groups.
- The approval demonstrated that DTx could meet the same regulatory rigor as drugs.

Marketing Lessons

1. **First-mover legitimacy:** Pear positioned reSET® not just as a product but as a proof-of-concept for the entire category of digital therapeutics.

2. **Regulatory approval as a marketing asset:** FDA clearance was leveraged as the ultimate trust builder with providers and payers.
3. **Bundling opportunity:** reSET® opened the door to drug–DTx combos (later seen in reSET-O® for opioid disorder with buprenorphine).
4. **Category education:** Success required not only marketing the product but also teaching stakeholders what a digital therapeutic even was.

Takeaway: reSET® wasn't just a product launch. It was a category launch. For pharma, it highlighted the power of DTx as partners to drugs—expanding therapeutic reach, engaging patients beyond clinic walls, and generating continuous data.

Case Study 2: Akili Interactive and EndeavorRx® – When Therapy Became a Video Game

Background

ADHD (Attention Deficit Hyperactivity Disorder) affects roughly 6 million children in the U.S. alone. Traditional treatment often combines behavioral therapy with stimulant medications. While effective, these approaches carry limitations: medications can cause side effects or parental hesitation, while behavioral therapy is resource-intensive and hard to access consistently. The unmet need was clear: a scalable, engaging, and evidence-based intervention that children would not resist but would instead embrace.

Challenge

The central challenge was engagement. How do you design therapy that a child wants to use on a daily basis? Traditional CBT modules felt too much like homework, and medication compliance was uneven. Clinicians were skeptical—how could playing on a screen qualify as "medicine"? Regulators, too, had never evaluated a product that appeared and felt like entertainment but claimed to have a clinical impact.

Intervention

Akili Interactive reframed the problem: what if therapy looked like fun? They designed EndeavorRx®, a prescription-only video game targeting neural pathways associated with attention.

- The game required children to multitask—dodging obstacles while responding to cues—tasks that have been shown to activate specific cognitive control networks.
- It was backed by rigorous clinical trials, enrolling hundreds of children with ADHD.
- Parents downloaded the game after receiving a physician's prescription, positioning it squarely as a form of medicine rather than entertainment.

Outcome

- In 2020, EndeavorRx became the first FDA-cleared video game-based therapeutic, marking a landmark achievement for both neurology and digital medicine.

- Clinical trials showed significant improvements in objective attention metrics, similar in size effect to some non-pharmacologic therapies.
- Families reported higher acceptance because children looked forward to using the therapy. Engagement was not a hurdle—it was the therapy.

Marketing Lessons

1. **Redefining medicine:** EndeavorRx forced stakeholders to expand their imagination of what constitutes therapy, opening doors for future "gamified" interventions.
2. **Parent trust is pivotal:** Marketing emphasized FDA approval and trial evidence, countering parental fears that this was "just a game."
3. **Engagement equals adherence:** Unlike pills, where refills measure adherence, DTx can hardwire engagement into the experience. For pharmaceutical marketers, this creates a new storytelling angle: adherence not as an obligation, but as a desire.
4. **Brand differentiation through novelty:** Akili's success demonstrates how bold, unconventional positioning can make a digital therapeutics (DTx) company stand out in crowded therapeutic areas.

Takeaway: EndeavorRx® didn't just treat ADHD—it reframed therapy itself. For the pharmaceutical industry, the case illustrates the potential of engagement-driven medicine, where design is as important as efficacy.

Case Study 3: Propeller Health – Turning Inhalers into Data Platforms

Background

Asthma and COPD are among the world's most common chronic respiratory conditions, affecting more than 500 million people globally. Medications exist that can control symptoms and reduce hospitalizations—yet adherence remains notoriously poor. Patients often forget doses, underestimate severity, or only use inhalers when symptoms flare. The result? Frequent ER visits, high costs, and preventable suffering.

By the mid-2010s, pharma companies faced a paradox: they had effective drugs, but poor patient adherence meant outcomes (and payer trust) lagged. Something beyond molecules was needed.

Challenge

The problem wasn't the drug. It was behavior. How do you ensure that patients use inhalers as prescribed, and how do you prove to payers that consistent use translates into fewer emergencies? Traditional marketing couldn't solve this—it needed real-world data. But adherence had always been invisible. Once a patient left the clinic, physicians and pharma lost sight of what happened.

Intervention

- Propeller Health developed a deceptively simple solution: a small Bluetooth sensor clipped onto inhalers.
- Each puff was recorded, timestamped, and linked to environmental data (like pollen or pollution).
- Patients received reminders and personalized feedback via a mobile app.
- Clinicians can view adherence dashboards and identify patients at risk.
- Payers gained access to aggregated outcomes, showing the impact of improved adherence on ER visits.

Crucially, Propeller integrated seamlessly—patients used their inhalers as before, with no new learning curve. The technology stayed invisible, while the data became invaluable.

Outcome

- Studies showed up to 58% reduction in ER visits for asthma patients using Propeller.
- Medication adherence improved significantly, with patients reporting greater confidence in managing their conditions.
- Pharma partners (like GSK and Novartis) leveraged Propeller to demonstrate real-world outcomes of their inhalers, differentiating themselves in competitive respiratory markets.
- Payers began recognizing Propeller-enabled inhalers as value-based care solutions, accelerating adoption.

Marketing Lessons

1. **Data as differentiation:** In categories where drugs are clinically similar, Propeller turned inhalers into data-generating platforms—a compelling marketing advantage.
2. **Invisible tech builds trust:** Adoption rose because Propeller required little behavior change. For DTx, simplicity is often more persuasive than sophistication.
3. **Payer proof over promotion:** Marketing shifted from glossy brochures to real-world outcomes, turning payer conversations from negotiation to collaboration.
4. **Brand halo effect:** Pharma brands associated with Propeller weren't just selling inhalers—they were seen as partners in patient health, reinforcing loyalty among physicians and patients alike.

Takeaway: Propeller Health didn't invent new drugs. It reinvented the value story around existing ones. For the pharmaceutical industry, it demonstrated that DTx can transform not just outcomes, but also how drugs are positioned, priced, and perceived.

Case Study 4: Omada Health – Redefining Prevention at Scale

Background

By the late 2000s, chronic diseases like diabetes, hypertension, and obesity had become the single largest burden on healthcare systems worldwide. In the U.S. alone, diabetes care consumed more than $300 billion annually. And yet, prevention remained elusive. Physicians could advise lifestyle changes, but follow-up was inconsistent, coaching resources were scarce, and patients often struggled alone between visits.

Public health experts knew that behavior change was the linchpin of prevention. The problem? Sustaining it. Traditional healthcare wasn't designed for continuous support.

Challenge

Insurers and employers had little incentive to pay for prevention. Outcomes were difficult to measure, cost savings were delayed, and interventions such as in-person coaching were expensive and challenging to scale.

For digital therapeutics to gain traction here, they had to prove two things simultaneously:

1. They worked clinically.
2. They saved money.

Without that dual proof, prevention programs would remain a "nice to have," not a reimbursed reality.

Intervention

Omada Health set out to digitize lifestyle medicine.

- Patients at risk of Type 2 diabetes enrolled in a digital program that combined weight tracking, step goals, nutrition logging, and human coaching delivered through an app.
- The program wasn't just about tracking data—it was about creating accountability loops. Coaches monitored progress, nudged patients, and celebrated small wins.
- Employers and insurers were offered a value proposition: fewer chronic disease cases down the line, fewer claims, and a healthier workforce.

Omada reframed prevention from "soft wellness" into hard healthcare economics.

Outcome

- Clinical trials and peer-reviewed studies have shown sustained weight loss and a reduced progression to Type 2 diabetes among participants.
- Independent evaluations found cost savings for employers and insurers, with reductions in long-term claims.
- Payers began reimbursing Omada programs, making it one of the first DTx companies to achieve widespread coverage in the U.S.
- Pharma companies took notice, exploring partnerships that bundled medications with Omada's digital programs for comorbid conditions.

Marketing Lessons

1. **Economics win payers:** Omada proved that prevention could move from theory to reimbursement only when it delivered measurable cost offsets.
2. **Behavioral science as brand story:** The program positioned itself not as an app but as a behavior-change engine—a narrative that resonated with both patients and payers.
3. **Employer partnerships as entry point:** By targeting self-insured employers, Omada bypassed payer hesitation and built a foundation of adoption.
4. **Blueprint for prevention DTx:** Omada showed that scalable prevention isn't about more clinics or staff—it's about digitally amplifying coaching and accountability.

Takeaway: Omada Health didn't just prevent diabetes—it changed the conversation around prevention itself. For pharma marketers, it illustrated how digital therapeutics can turn long-term, intangible outcomes into concrete, billable value propositions.

Case Study 5: Kaia Health – Scaling Physiotherapy Through AI

Background

Chronic back pain is the leading cause of disability worldwide, responsible for billions in lost productivity and healthcare costs. Clinical guidelines recommend physiotherapy and exercise as first-line treatments. But in practice, access to qualified physiotherapists is uneven—scarce in rural areas, expensive in urban ones, and often limited by long wait times. Millions of patients rely instead on painkillers, which offer temporary relief but carry risks of dependency and side effects.

The unmet need was glaring: how do you deliver high-quality, personalized physiotherapy at scale?

Challenge

Traditional physiotherapy is resource-intensive. Patients need one-on-one supervision to ensure correct posture, safe progression, and consistent adherence. Scaling that model digitally posed a paradox:

- Could an app really replace the watchful eye of a therapist?
- Would patients trust a smartphone to guide movements that could either heal or harm?
- Could insurers see enough value in digital physiotherapy to cover it?

For Kaia Health, solving these challenges meant blending clinical rigor with cutting-edge technology.

Intervention

Kaia Health developed a smartphone-based program for managing back pain and later expanded it to include COPD. Its key innovation was AI-powered motion tracking:

- Using a smartphone camera, the app guided patients through exercises, offering real-time feedback on form and posture—mimicking the corrective role of a physiotherapist.
- The program integrated education, mindfulness, and breathing modules to address both physical and psychological dimensions of chronic pain.
- Clinicians could monitor patient progress through dashboards, bridging the gap between in-person and digital care.

- Partnerships with health insurers in Europe and the U.S. helped integrate Kaia into care pathways.

Outcome

- Clinical trials have demonstrated significant reductions in back pain severity and improvements in function, often comparable to those achieved through in-person physiotherapy.
- Adherence improved as patients appreciated the convenience and flexibility of training at home.
- Health insurers in Germany and the U.S. began covering Kaia's program, citing its ability to reduce long-term costs associated with chronic pain and absenteeism.
- Pharma companies in musculoskeletal therapy areas explored partnerships to bundle Kaia with pain management drugs.

Marketing Lessons

1. **Technology as therapist:** Kaia showed that AI and computer vision can deliver not just engagement but clinical accuracy—positioning tech as a trusted clinical partner.
2. **Holistic positioning:** By combining exercise with mindfulness and education, Kaia marketed itself not just as a digital physiotherapy tool, but as a comprehensive pain management solution.
3. **Convenience as value:** Patients embraced Kaia because it fit into daily life—an insight marketers can leverage by highlighting usability as much as outcomes.
4. **Payer engagement through data:** Real-world evidence of reduced healthcare utilization helped Kaia secure reimbursement, underscoring the importance of economic storytelling in digital therapeutics (DTx) marketing.

Takeaway: Kaia Health demonstrated that AI can scale scarce clinical resources without compromising quality. For pharmaceutical marketers, the lesson is that digital therapeutics can amplify drug value by addressing both the behavioral and physical dimensions of disease—turning products into ecosystems.

Case Study 6: Deprexis – Extending Mental Health Care in Europe

Background

Depression is among the most widespread health conditions worldwide, with the World Health Organization estimating more than 280 million people affected. In Europe, the challenge has been particularly acute: access to qualified therapists is limited, waiting lists stretch for months, and stigma continues to keep many from seeking face-to-face care. By the mid-2000s, the gap between those who needed therapy and those who received it had become a silent crisis.

Challenge

Cognitive Behavioral Therapy (CBT) is one of the most evidence-based treatments for depression. Yet availability remained uneven. Patients in rural Germany or France might have to wait months for therapy, while urban clinics faced overwhelming demand. How could a clinically validated form of therapy be delivered at scale without diluting its quality?

Moreover, skepticism was high. Could a computer-based program ever replicate the nuanced guidance of a human therapist? Would patients trust digital modules with their most personal struggles?

Intervention

- Deprexis, developed in Germany, was one of the first fully validated digital CBT programs for depression.
- The software delivered personalized, interactive CBT modules that adapted to patient responses.
- It was designed to be accessible anytime, anywhere, offering immediate support rather than waiting months for an appointment.
- Patients could use it as a stand-alone intervention or as a bridge between face-to-face therapy sessions.
- Clinical studies were conducted across Europe, comparing Deprexis outcomes to traditional therapy.

Outcome

Multiple randomized controlled trials showed that Deprexis significantly reduced depressive symptoms, often achieving outcomes comparable to face-to-face CBT.

- In Germany, insurers began reimbursing Deprexis under digital health frameworks, expanding access nationwide.
- For many patients, Deprexis became their first experience of structured therapy, reducing stigma by offering privacy and discretion.
- The program also provided a model for scalable, clinically validated digital therapeutic (DTx) for mental health, paving the way for successors like SilverCloud and Woebot.

Marketing Lessons

1. **Legitimacy through evidence:** Deprexis positioned itself not as a "self-help app" but as a validated therapy, publishing results in peer-reviewed journals—a model all DTx marketers should emulate.
2. **Access as value proposition:** Marketing emphasized how Deprexis could close gaps in systems with long wait times, making access itself the product's differentiator.
3. **Adjunct framing builds trust:** By presenting itself as a complement, not competitor, to therapists, Deprexis eased provider concerns and boosted adoption.
4. **Privacy as engagement driver:** In mental health, discretion matters. Deprexis leveraged privacy as a benefit, helping patients overcome stigma barriers.

Takeaway: Deprexis demonstrated that digital therapeutics can democratize access to mental health care without compromising clinical rigor. For pharma, it illustrated how DTx can complement existing care ecosystems and expand treatment reach—turning access gaps into market opportunities.

Case Study 7: SilverCloud Health – The Hybrid Model of Digital Therapy

Background

Mental health services across the U.K. and Ireland were under immense strain by the 2010s. The NHS reported ballooning waiting lists for therapy, while patients with depression and anxiety often had to wait weeks—or months—for care. Digital self-help apps existed, but many lacked clinical validation. What was needed was a middle path: something scalable yet trustworthy, digital yet still anchored in human oversight.

Challenge

Mental health interventions walk a delicate line. Patients want access and convenience, as well as empathy and safety. Could a digital tool scale without feeling cold or impersonal? And would clinicians trust a system that eliminated face-to-face contact as the primary means of therapy?

Intervention

SilverCloud Health pioneered a hybrid model: digital CBT modules combined with optional human therapist "check-ins."

- The platform provided structured CBT programs for depression, anxiety, stress, and chronic illness support.
- Patients worked independently through digital modules, but clinicians could review progress and send supportive messages.
- By balancing automation with human touch, SilverCloud made therapy more scalable while preserving trust.

Outcome

- Multiple RCTs showed that SilverCloud achieved symptom reduction comparable to face-to-face therapy.
- The NHS adopted SilverCloud, embedding it into its Improving Access to Psychological Therapies (IAPT) program.
- Expansion into the U.S. and other markets followed, proving global scalability.
- Patients appreciated both the autonomy and the reassurance of knowing a human was still in the loop.

Marketing Lessons

1. **Hybrid is credible:** Positioning DTx as a supplement rather than replacement reassured providers and encouraged adoption.
2. **Institutional partnerships matter:** NHS endorsement gave SilverCloud legitimacy and visibility—showing how alignment with healthcare systems accelerates scale.
3. **Empathy as differentiator:** Marketing emphasized "supported digital therapy," reframing SilverCloud not as cold automation but as augmented human care.
4. **Scalability with trust:** By blending self-guided and clinician-supported modes, SilverCloud proved you don't have to sacrifice human trust to gain efficiency.

Takeaway: SilverCloud demonstrated that the future of DTx doesn't have to be binary (human vs. digital). For the pharmaceutical industry, it offered a model of how digital therapeutics can be packaged as hybrid care solutions, attractive to both patients and healthcare systems.

Case Study 8: Happify Health – Gamified Engagement Meets Pharma Partnership

Background

The global mental wellness market is flooded with mindfulness and mood apps, but most lack clinical evidence. Happify Health sought to bridge the gap by creating a platform that combined gamified CBT and mindfulness exercises with clinical validation. Its ambition went further: to partner with pharma in supporting patients with chronic conditions where mental health was a hidden burden.

Challenge

How do you differentiate a clinically validated product in a sea of wellness apps? And how do you convince pharma companies that digital mental health tools aren't just "nice extras" but strategic assets in brand positioning?

Intervention

Happify Health created digital programs blending science-backed CBT and positive psychology with gamification to sustain engagement.

- Patients interacted with exercises framed as games, reinforcing positive thought patterns.
- The company pursued rigorous clinical validation and peer-reviewed publication to stand apart from consumer wellness apps.
- Crucially, Happify forged partnerships with pharma companies like Sanofi, embedding its programs as companions to drug therapies (e.g., in multiple sclerosis and immunology).

Outcome

- Clinical trials showed reductions in depression and anxiety symptoms.
- Pharma collaborations expanded Happify's reach, positioning it not just as an app but as a strategic therapeutic add-on.
- Patients appreciated the playful, engaging design—especially those dealing with the mental health burdens of chronic illness.

Marketing Lessons

Engagement as clinical value: Happify turned fun into medicine, proving gamification isn't fluff but a therapeutic tool.

1. **Pharma partnerships as multipliers:** By embedding within pharma portfolios, Happify reached patients that pharma brands already served.
2. **Differentiation through science:** Validation separated Happify from thousands of unregulated wellness apps, making it marketable to providers and payers.
3. **Emotional resonance:** Marketing emphasized joy and positivity—a fresh approach in an often clinical and serious healthcare landscape.

Takeaway: Happify demonstrated that emotional design and gamification, when supported by evidence, can both enhance outcomes and strengthen pharmaceutical brand strategies.

Case Study 9: CureApp – Japan's Digital Prescription for Smoking Cessation

Background

Smoking-related illnesses cost Japan billions annually in healthcare expenditures. Traditional cessation programs—counseling, nicotine replacement, medication—helped some but fell short for many. With high relapse rates, Japan's Ministry of Health sought new approaches.

Challenge

How do you create a scalable cessation program that doesn't just inform patients but sustains behavior change? And how do you persuade regulators—long accustomed to drugs and devices—that an app can be prescribed like a medicine?

Intervention

Japanese start-up CureApp developed a DTx app for smoking cessation.

- It combined digital CBT modules with personalized messages and reminders.
- Patients used it alongside nicotine replacement therapy, reinforcing habits between clinic visits.
- CureApp worked closely with the Japanese Ministry of Health to secure approval.

Outcome

- In 2020, CureApp's smoking cessation digital therapeutic (DTx) became the first government-approved prescription app in Japan.
- Trials showed higher quit rates compared to standard care.
- Its success encouraged broader acceptance of DTx in Asia, with CureApp expanding into areas such as hypertension.

Marketing Lessons

1. **Government partnership is key:** CureApp's early collaboration with regulators ensured a smoother approval process.
2. **Behavioral reinforcement sells:** Marketing emphasized how the app kept patients motivated between clinical visits.

3. **Gateway product strategy:** Smoking cessation became a visible "win," building credibility for CureApp's expansion into other conditions.
4. **Asia-Pacific leadership:** CureApp positioned Japan as a global pioneer in DTx regulation, opening opportunities in neighboring markets.

Takeaway: CureApp proved that DTx could succeed in Asia, creating a model for partnerships with regulators and insurers in markets beyond Europe and the U.S.

Case Study 10: Click Therapeutics – Prescription-Only Software in the U.S.

Background

Click Therapeutics emerged as a leader in the U.S. digital therapeutics (DTx) space, focusing on developing prescription-only software for psychiatric and neurological conditions. Its vision: software validated in trials, reimbursed by insurers, and prescribed like any other therapy.

Challenge

The market was crowded with mental health apps, most unregulated. Click had to carve a distinct identity as a serious medical company while navigating payer skepticism.

Intervention

Click developed a portfolio of DTx for major depressive disorder, smoking cessation, and migraine.

- Programs were designed for prescription use only, reinforcing legitimacy.
- The company partnered with major pharmaceutical companies (e.g., Otsuka, Boehringer Ingelheim) to co-develop digital therapeutics alongside their traditional pipelines.
- Heavy investment in clinical trials underscored its evidence-first strategy.

Outcome

- Multiple products progressed through clinical trials, with FDA submissions underway.
- Partnerships with pharmaceutical companies provided Click with revenue stability and access to payer networks.
- By branding itself as "the prescription digital therapeutics company," Click created category clarity.

Marketing Lessons

1. **Brand positioning matters:** Click's insistence on being "prescription-only" differentiated it from consumer wellness apps.
2. **Partnerships build credibility:** Collaborating with pharma provided validation and commercialization strength.

3. **Pipeline strategy mirrors pharma:** By building a portfolio across conditions, Click signaled long-term seriousness, not one-hit wonder.
4. **Evidence-first marketing:** Positioning trials as proof points helped convince skeptical payers.

Takeaway: Click Therapeutics demonstrates how DTx companies can evolve into pharmaceutical-like entities, featuring robust pipelines, strategic partnerships, and rigorous regulatory oversight.

Patterns Across Case Studies

1. Regulatory legitimacy (FDA, CE, DiGA, MHLW) = trust & adoption.
2. Engagement as therapy (Akili, Happify) sustains adherence.
3. Data as currency (Propeller, Omada) drives payer decisions.
4. Hybrid & adjunct framing (SilverCloud, Deprexis) eases provider concerns.
5. Partnerships with pharma (Click, Happify, Omada) accelerate commercialization.

Closing Thought

These case studies show digital therapeutics aren't abstract innovations—they are living experiments in how code becomes care. Each one reflects a lesson: legitimacy, engagement, economics, empathy, or partnerships. For pharmaceutical marketers, they serve as both a playbook and a benchmarking tool, helping them decide where to invest, how to position their products, and how to build trust.

Appendix E

Additional Reading and References

Every new field needs its "canon"—the works that shape thinking, frame debates, and guide practice. Digital therapeutics, still a relatively young field, already has a well-established canon. It encompasses regulatory white papers, market analyses, academic trials, and thought leadership essays. This appendix curates the most essential resources, each explained not just as what it is, but why it matters.

1. **Regulatory and Policy Resources**
    - FDA – Digital Health Innovation Action Plan (2017)
    - Why it matters: The first formal signal from the FDA that digital health and therapeutics would be regulated seriously, laying the foundation for the SaMD (Software as a Medical Device) framework.
    - European Commission – Medical Device Regulation (MDR) Guidelines (2021 update)
    - Why it matters: Defines how digital therapeutics achieve CE Marking in Europe. Crucial for marketers entering EU markets.
    - Germany's BfArM DiGA Directory
    - Why it matters: The world's first national reimbursement catalogue for DTx. A living blueprint of which digital therapeutics insurers cover and why.
    - Japan Ministry of Health, Labour and Welfare (MHLW) – CureApp Approval Announcement (2020)

    Why it matters: A case study in Asia's regulatory leadership, showing how non-Western frameworks are emerging.
2. **Academic & Clinical Evidence**
    - Nature Digital Medicine – Peer-reviewed journal articles on digital therapeutics.

- Why it matters: Provides gold-standard scientific validation, separating hype from proven outcomes.
- JAMA Psychiatry (2020) "Effect of a Prescription Digital Therapeutic for Insomnia on Clinical Outcomes"
- Why it matters: Landmark RCT supporting Somryst®. Shows how DTx can rival gold-standard face-to-face therapy.
- Lancet Digital Health "Gamified Interventions for Cognitive Disorders" (2021)
- Why it matters: Evidence underpinning EndeavorRx® and the gamification trend.
- BMJ (British Medical Journal) "Digital Health Interventions in Chronic Disease Management"
- Why it matters: Synthesizes how digital therapeutics (DTx) are transforming care for diabetes, COPD, and hypertension.

3. **Industry and Market Analyses**

   - Rock Health – Digital Health Funding Reports (annual)

     Why it matters: Tracks venture capital trends, showing where investors believe the future lies.

   - IQVIA Institute "Digital Health Trends" Reports

     Why it matters: Essential data on adoption rates, reimbursement models, and global DTx usage.

   - Deloitte Insights "The Future of Digital Therapeutics" (2022)

     Why it matters: Explains commercial strategies, payer alignment, and pharma partnership models.

   - Frost & Sullivan – Market Forecasts for DTx (global)

     Why it matters: Quantifies the market opportunity and competitive landscape.

4. **Case Studies and Company Resources**

   - Pear Therapeutics White Papers

     Why it matters: Illustrates how a pioneer in the space communicates with payers and regulators.

- Akili Interactive Clinical Trial Summaries

  Why it matters: Showcases the rigor behind FDA-cleared gamified therapies.

- Omada Health Outcomes Reports

  Why it matters: Concrete evidence that prevention can deliver measurable ROI for payers.

- Propeller Health Case Studies (with GSK & Novartis)

  Why it matters: Proof that pharma–DTx partnerships can generate new value stories.

5. **Books and Broader Context**

   - Eric Topol "Deep Medicine" (2019)

     Why it matters: Frames how AI and digital health are reshaping medicine.

   - Brennan Spiege "VRx: How Virtual Therapeutics Will Revolutionize Medicine" (2020)

     Why it matters: A deep dive into immersive therapeutics, a frontier of DTx.

   - Eyal Zimlichman et al. "Handbook of Digital Health"

     Why it matters: A comprehensive overview of the field, often used in academia.

Closing Thought

These references are more than footnotes. They are the scaffolding on which the field of digital therapeutics is being built. For pharma marketers, they provide the evidence, frameworks, and foresight needed to move from curiosity to conviction.

The lesson is simple: the more you read, the more you see that digital therapeutics are not just an emerging niche—they are the next chapter of medicine.

Bibliography

Academic & Clinical Evidence

1. Becker, E. M., & Jensen-Doss, A. (2019). Computer-assisted therapies for mental health problems in children and adolescents: A systematic review. Journal of Child Psychology and Psychiatry, 60(12), 1325–1336.
2. Bickmore, T. W., & Picard, R. W. (2020). Establishing and maintaining long-term human–computer relationships. ACM Transactions on Computer-Human Interaction, 26(6), 1–20.
3. Espie, C. A., Luik, A. I., Cape, J., et al. (2019). Digital cognitive behavioural therapy for insomnia versus sleep hygiene education: a randomized controlled trial. JAMA Psychiatry, 76(1), 21–30.
4. Kvedar, J., Fogel, A. L., & Elenko, E. (2016). Digital medicine's march on chronic disease. Nature Biotechnology, 34(3), 239–246.
5. Thase, M. E., McCrone, P., Barrett, M. S., et al. (2018). Improving access to psychological therapies with Internet interventions: Results from the Deprexis program. Cognitive Behaviour Therapy, 47(2), 109–126.
6. Wykes, T., & Schueller, S. M. (2019). Why reviewing apps is not enough: Transparency for trust (T4T) principles of responsible health app marketplaces. Journal of Medical Internet Research, 21(5), e12390.

Regulatory & Policy Documents

7. European Commission. (2021). Medical Device Regulation (MDR): Guidance for Software as a Medical Device. Brussels: European Union.
8. Federal Institute for Drugs and Medical Devices (BfArM). (2020). DiGA Fast-Track Guidance for Digital Health Applications. Bonn: BfArM.
9. Food and Drug Administration (FDA). (2017). Digital Health Innovation Action Plan. Washington, DC: U.S. FDA.

10. Food and Drug Administration (FDA). (2019). Software as a Medical Device (SaMD): Clinical Evaluation Guidance. Washington, DC: U.S. FDA.

11. Ministry of Health, Labour and Welfare (MHLW), Japan. (2020). Approval of Digital Therapeutic App for Smoking Cessation (CureApp). Tokyo: Government of Japan.

12. National Institute for Health and Care Excellence (NICE). (2022). Evidence Standards Framework for Digital Health Technologies. London: NICE.

Industry & Market Reports

13. Deloitte Insights. (2022). The Future of Digital Therapeutics: Commercial Strategies for Pharma and Payers. Deloitte Consulting LLP.

14. Frost & Sullivan. (2021). Global Digital Therapeutics Market Forecast to 2030. Frost & Sullivan Market Report.

15. IQVIA Institute for Human Data Science. (2021). Digital Health Trends 2021: Innovation, Evidence, Regulation, and Adoption. Durham, NC: IQVIA.

16. Rock Health. (2022). Digital Health Funding Report. San Francisco: Rock Health.

17. Topol, E. (2019). Deep Medicine: How Artificial Intelligence Can Make Healthcare Human Again. New York: Basic Books.

18. Spiegel, B. (2020). VRx: How Virtual Therapeutics Will Revolutionize Medicine. New York: Basic Books.

Closing Note

This bibliography blends academic rigor (peer-reviewed trials), policy frameworks (FDA, EMA, DiGA, NICE), and industry foresight (IQVIA, Deloitte, Rock Health). For pharma marketers and healthcare professionals, it provides the three dimensions needed to navigate digital therapeutics: science, regulation, and strategy.

About the Author

Subba Rao Chaganti

He has a master's in business administration and over fifty-two years of experience in

Pharmaceutical marketing. His experience encompasses all facets of the industry, from sales and sales management to product management and overseeing overall marketing activities. He has experience in both domestic and international marketing, as well as within the Indian and multinational sectors.

He also taught a course on Advertising and Brand Management as an adjunct professor at Gitam Institute of Foreign Trade (now part of Gitam University) in Visakhapatnam for a few years and a course on Marketing as a visiting faculty member at Jawaharlal Nehru Technological University (JNTU) in Hyderabad.

He lives in Farmington, Connecticut, USA, and can be reached at: subbarao.chaganti@gmail.com.

Here is a list of his publications:

1. Pharmaceutical Marketing in India: Concepts, Cases, Strategy
2. Game Plans for Post-GATT Era: Action Agenda of the Indian Pharmaceutical Industry
3. Compete or Forfeit: Strategies for Sustainable Competitive Advantage in the Pharma Product Patents Era
4. Pharmaceutical Marketing in India for Today and Tomorrow - 25th Anniversary Edition
5. Bullseyes and Blunders: Lessons from 100 Cases in Pharma Marketing
6. Digital Pharma Marketing Playbook: Winning With the New Rules of Engagement
7. Cracking the Generics Code: Your Single-Source Success Manual for Winning in Multi-Source Product Markets
8. Reimagine Pharma Marketing: Make It Future-Proof!
9. Brand Positioning in Pharma

10. Transactional to Transformational Marketing in Pharma: The Science of Why and The Art of How
11. A to Z of Pharmaceutical Marketing: World's First and Only Encyclopedia in Two Volumes
12. The Synergy of Minds: Human+AI Orchestrating the Pharma Marketing Revolution
13. Design Thinking for Pharma
14. The Pharma Product Manager: Navigating the Digital Frontier
15. Sentiment Analysis for Pharma Marketers
16. Whispering to AI: Prompt Engineering for Pharma Brand Managers
17. Storytelling in Pharma Marketing
18. Beyond the Molecule: The Art and Science of Metaphors That Matter
19. The Voices Within: Your Body Speaks When Your Organs Tell Their Own Stories
20. Pharma Archetypes: The Science of Meaningful Healthcare Marketing
21. Navigating the AI Revolution: Human Futures
22. Breaking Through: A Business Novel (based on the theory of constraints)
23. The Wearable Edge: Redefining Pharma Marketing in a Connected and Data-Driven World

www.ingramcontent.com/pod-product-compliance
Lightning Source LLC
Chambersburg PA
CBHW071444230926
51846CB00001B/341